Timex/Sinclair User's Guide

Volume 1

Joseph C. Giarratano

Que Corporation

Indianapolis

Cover art: Dick Held
Illustrations: Linda Holman
Photography: Jonathan Mangin
Design: Paul Mangin
Typeset in Helvetica by Alexander Typesetting, Inc.

Manufactured in the United States of America

Published by Que Corporation
7960 Castleway Drive
Indianapolis, Indiana 46250

About the Author

Joseph C. Giarratano received his B.S. and M.S. degrees in physics from California State University at Los Angeles. In 1974 he earned his Ph.D. degree in physics at the University of Texas at Austin.

Dr. Giarratano has worked in the field of medical physics with interests in the applications of computers to medicine. He now works in the area of software development for microprocessor-based products.

Dr. Giarratano is also the author of four other books on computers: *Foundations of Computer Technology, Modern Computer Concepts, BASIC: Fundamental Concepts,* and *BASIC: Advanced Concepts.* The first two books cover computer technology, and the latter two are about programming in Microsoft BASIC and Digital Equipment Corp. BASIC.

Editorial Director

David F. Noble, Ph.D.

Editors

Diane F. Brown, M.A.
Virginia D. Noble, M.L.S.

Managing Editor

Paul L. Mangin

TABLE OF CONTENTS

Preface

Do you hear a lot about computers and want to know more about them? Have you been putting off learning about computers? Are you just waiting for the 'prices to come down' before you make an effort to learn about computers?

If you've answered yes to any of these questions, then the Timex/Sinclair 1000 computer is for you, and this book, the *Timex/Sinclair 1000 User's Guide,* Volume 1, is also for you. The two together can introduce you to the world of computers.
The T/S 1000 is a very versatile computer and not just a glorified calculator. Que's *User's Guide* is designed to lead you step by step into computer programming with the T/S 1000 so that you may personally enter the Computer Age.

This book is designed for people who know little about computers, but who want to learn how to program a computer. By working through this book side by side with your T/S 1000 computer, you will learn what a computer does, how to control the computer, and how to program in the BASIC computer language. This easy-to-learn, but powerful, language has been used to teach programming to hundreds of thousands of people from children to adults. Teachers, students, business people, and many others have found learning about computers to be an enjoyable and rewarding experience.

This book is the first volume of two new books by Que about the T/S 1000 computer. These books will show you how to write practical and entertaining programs. In this first volume, you will learn how to use the T/S 1000 as a simple calculator, next as a super-calculator, and then as a computer that runs programs. You will learn how to write your own programs and run prerecorded programs. You will be shown how useful the computer can be in comparison shopping for mortgages, figuring an Individual Retirement Account, and many other practical and educational applications. In addition, you'll see how much fun the computer can be in creating your own games.

In the *Timex/Sinclair 1000 User's Guide*, Volume 2, you can continue your study of computers with more advanced commands. You will see applications to store checkbook information, plot graphics, and program video games. You will also be introduced to machine language.

Both volumes are *practical* guides, giving you many tips on how to program efficiently to save memory space. Many of the things you'll learn about programming in these volumes can be applied to your work, school, hobbies, and personal enjoyment.

The topics covered in these books progress in easy stages from elementary to advanced applications. Each chapter serves as a solid foundation for the next. Whatever your age or occupation may be, you *can* learn about computers, if you work at it.

Like learning any language, you'll find it easiest if you practice every day. As your skill and knowledge increase, you will see why the computer is the greatest tool that has ever been invented. Best of all, you'll see how *you* can benefit from the computer.

CHAPTER 1
Introduction to Computers

Today, there are many reasons for buying a computer. If you want to

- Save money
- Save time
- Get organized
- Eliminate boring and repetitious calculation
- Improve your efficiency
- Become better educated about the world of computers
- Enjoy games that challenge your intelligence as well as your reflexes

then a computer may be just the answer.

Also, there is a good reason for buying a Timex/Sinclair 1000 computer: it gives you the most power for the least money. The T/S 1000 is the lowest priced computer you can buy and a great tool for learning how to program.

Buying a Computer

What can you do with a computer? Anything it can be taught or programmed to do. The T/S 1000 will obey a sequence of instructions, called a program. Different programs will make your computer do different things. For example, there are programs available to

- Balance your checkbook
- Calculate taxes
- Organize your records, recipes, or any collection
- Educate people of all ages
- Play games

—and just about anything else you can think of. The best thing about a computer is that you can make it become anything you want simply by changing its program. Unlike most calculators, which can't be programmed, the T/S 1000 lets you change it

from a game machine,

to an educational machine,

to a business machine,

to a personal and home machine,

just by altering the program stored in its memory.

You can get programs for your computer in several ways:

1. Buy them
2. Copy them from magazines or books
3. Make up your own

Examples of some programs available for purchase are shown in Chapter 2.

Anyone who owns a video game machine is familiar with purchased programs. The game cartridge you plug into the machine contains the program that tells the computer what to do. The instructions in the game cartridge are programmed or stored into the computer's memory. When you remove the game cartridge, the computer forgets what it has learned—that is, the contents of its memory are erased.

A big difference between the T/S 1000 and a game computer is that the game machine only plays games someone else has written. Magazines like *Sync* and *Syntax* regularly carry ads from companies and people who developed programs for their own computers. In fact, people have made money selling programs they have created in their spare time.

Unlike common video games, the T/S 1000 allows you to create your own game programs. You write the programs in an easy-to-learn, but powerful, computer language called BASIC. You can also write programs to handle your finances, calculate taxes, and do many other applications.

Today, the world is changing faster and faster. Learning about computers and programming will help you prepare for, and keep up with, all these changes. Best of all, learning about computers is fun. It is like learning to ride a bicycle: once you've started, you'll be amazed at how easy it is.

Setting up the Timex/Sinclair 1000

Like a video game, the T/S 1000 has to be hooked up to a TV so that you can see what the computer is doing. To help you connect the computer to the TV, Figure 1-1 shows a photo of the T/S 1000's parts.

The TV Switch Box

The cable from the jack labeled "TV" goes to the switch box. Notice that it looks just like the switch box for a video game. The T/S 1000 switch box allows you to use your TV for regular viewing when you're not using the computer. Move the switch to "TV" when you want to watch regular TV programs, or to "Computer" when you want to use the computer. Either a black and white or color TV can be used. The computer puts out only a black and white TV picture, and it may look better on a black and white set.

Figure 1-2 shows a photo of how the switch box is connected to the TV. Be sure the switch is on "Computer."

Figure 1-1
*The Timex/Sinclair 1000 computer comes with accessories shown below:
Power supply and cord, TV switch box, TV connector cable, and
cassette connector cable.*

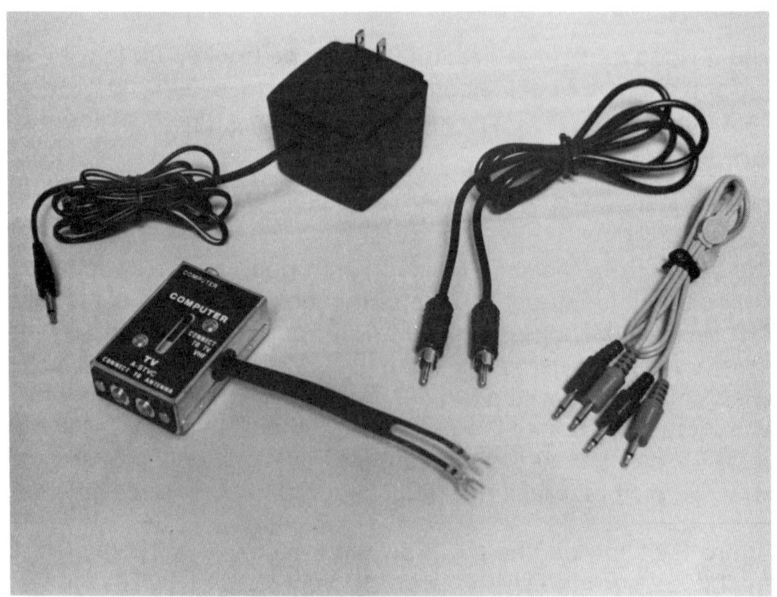

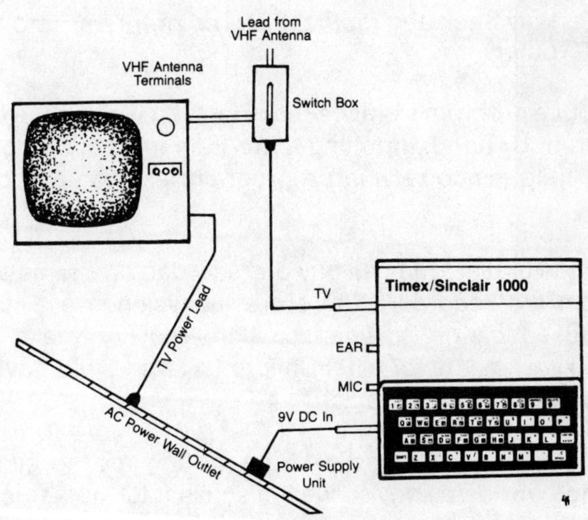

Figure 1-2
Connecting the T/S 1000 to your television set.

The Computer's TV Channel Switch

Now, turn the computer over and look at its bottom, as shown in Figure 1-4. Notice the switch marked CH2-CH3. If you push the switch to CH2, the output of the T/S 1000 will be on channel 2 of your TV. Likewise, if you move the switch to CH3, you'll see the output on channel 3. Use whichever channel is unused for TV in your area. Otherwise, you'll get interference on the TV screen, and you may interfere with your neighbors' reception.

The Cassette Recorder

The cable labeled "Cassette Recorder" connects the T/S 1000 to an ordinary cassette recorder, which is convenient to use for saving and loading programs on tape. Figure 1-3 shows how the recorder is connected. Just about any cassette recorder should work. The cassette recorder can do two things:

    1. *"Output"* and store your programs from the T/S 1000 onto cassettes

2. Play back and *input* the stored programs into the computer

If you input a program from the recorder, you won't have to type in the program by hand. Inputting a program from the recorder can be a big help, since retyping a program takes time and can be tedious.

As indicated earlier, you can buy prerecorded programs and input them from the recorder. There are many kinds available from games, to education, to finance. Also, you can make tapes of programs you create for sale. Children 11 years old have written and sold their own programs!

For a while, the programs we'll be writing are so simple that they're not worth saving; so we'll discuss later how to save programs with a cassette recorder.

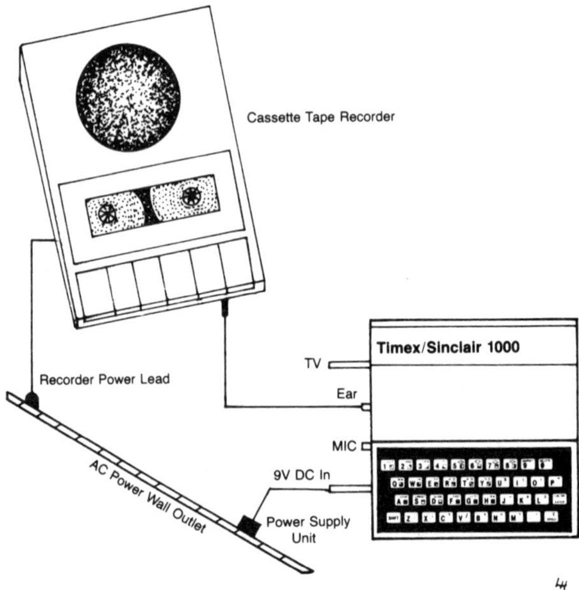

Figure 1-3
Connecting the T/S 1000 to your cassette tape recorder.

Figure 1-4
The channel selector switch.

The Power Cord

The last item you'll notice in Figure 1-1 is the power cord. Just plug it into an ordinary wall socket to power the computer. Inserting the plug is how you turn on the computer. Pulling out the plug is one way to turn off the computer. The power cord plugs into the computer jack labeled "9V D.C." You can also turn off the computer by unplugging the power cord from this jack. Removing the cord will erase the contents of the computer's memory. Therefore, be careful not to unplug the cord from the jack unless you really want to.

When you're done using the computer for a while, it is best to unplug it from the wall, or turn off the power through an extra power cord switch. Although only 9 volts D.C. come through the power plug, it's not a good idea to leave live voltage around, even if it is as low as 9 volts.

Some other brands of computers have an ON/OFF switch so that you don't have to plug and unplug the power cord. You can easily buy a line cord with an ON/OFF switch to plug in the power cord,

Figure 1-5
This screen image indicates that you are ready to start.

Using such a switch is much more convenient than plugging and unplugging the power cord from the wall socket.

Adjusting the Screen

Once you've connected the T/S 1000 to the TV, the cassette recorder, and the wall socket, turn on the TV, turn down the volume all the way, and watch the screen. If you have followed each step correctly, you should see the output as shown in Figure 1-5. The screen should be blank except for a little **K** in the bottom left corner.

If you don't see this kind of picture, the solution is easy. Just turn the fine tuning knob of your TV set until you get a picture like the one in Figure 1-5. If there are wavy lines in the picture, try adjusting the brightness and contrast controls for the clearest picture.

If you don't see anything like Figure 1-5, check to be certain that the channel setting of your TV matches the channel switch setting on the bottom of your T/S 1000. If you can't get a good picture on either channel 2 or 3, try another TV set. If that fails, there may be a problem with the computer. Just take it back to the store where you bought it.

If any letters or symbols other than **K** appear on the screen, they probably are there because you accidentally touched the computer keyboard while fine tuning the TV. To get rid of them, unplug the power cord, then plug it in again.

For the best picture, you may wish to make a little circuit for *direct video output.* The T/S 1000 provides a radio frequency (RF) output to drive your TV antenna. However, some TVs have a direct video *input.* Your T/S 1000 produces a video output that is then converted to RF by a circuit inside the computer. However, the best picture results from using the video output directly without RF conversion.

If you or a friend is handy with electronics, you can make the simple circuit referred to in one of the references of Appendix A. The circuit was designed originally for a Sinclair ZX-81, but the T/S 1000 is almost identical to the Sinclair ZX-81. The only difference is that the T/S 1000 has twice the memory of the ZX-81.

Using such a circuit, you can't drive a TV set by its antenna. The TV set must have a *composite video input,* or you must use a *video monitor.* Also, note that *if you modify your T/S 1000, any change voids the warranty.*

CHAPTER 2
Getting Loaded

One of the best features of the T/S 1000 computer is its ability to save and load programs. Using an ordinary cassette recorder, you can save on cassette tape any programs you've written. You can then load them back into the computer and run them just as if you had typed them. Also, you can buy dozens of prerecorded tapes of games and business, educational, and personal programs. However, before buying prerecorded tapes, find out how much memory their programs need. Prerecorded cassettes indicate how much memory is needed to run them.

Memory Requirements

Some programs on tape need 16K bytes of memory instead of the standard 2K bytes that come with the T/S 1000. To run a 16K-byte program, you'll have to buy a 16K random access memory (RAM) Module for your computer. The 16K RAM Module expands your computer's memory by eight times and allows you to store more data and run much longer programs. For example, the 16K RAM Module is useful for a check balancing program, as described later in this book. With 16K of RAM, you can easily store and retrieve data on hundreds of checks.

Prerecorded Programs

The following are descriptions of some prerecorded cassettes from Timex. The tapes are arranged by their applications, and memory requirements are given after each title. Other tapes are commonly advertised in magazines like *Syntax* and *Sync*.

INTRODUCTORY

The Starter™ - 2K

Part of the tape is the Game of Life, which generates on the screen patterns that simulate the growth of cells. Another part is Maths, a program with drills on addition, subtraction, multiplication, and division. A third program is called Averages. It computes the mean and median of data, then draws a bar chart on the screen.

ENTERTAINMENT

Backgammon™ - 16K

Two programs are on this tape: Backgammon and a Dice program. The Dice program is not a game, but simulates the rolling of dice for any game that needs dice.

The Cube Game™ - 16K

This program is Rubik's Cube for the computer.

The Gambler™ - 16K

This tape has two programs: Blackjack and Slot Machine.

PERSONAL

The Budgeter™ - 16K

The Budgeter helps you to create and maintain a home budget. You can enter expenses in up to 18 different categories. The computer keeps track of your expenses and shows the money available in each category. All of the budget information can be saved on tape.

The Carpooler™ - 16K

With The Carpooler you can manage a car pool by scheduling drivers, riders, vehicles, and departure times.

The Coupon Manager™ - 16K

This program organizes coupons. It allows up to 18 different kinds of coupons and keeps track of both their acceptance dates and the stores that will accept the coupons.

The Stamp Collector™ - 16K

The Stamp Collector allows you to manage a stamp collection. You can (1) add and delete stamps, (2) search for stamps by ID number or by classification code, and (3) display the stamps you want. You can store all U.S. stamps on three cassette tapes.

PERSONAL/BUSINESS

The Checkbook Manager™ - 16K

This program allows your computer to store, retrieve, and sort information about banking transactions. You can store up to 250 deposits or issued checks, then retrieve the data (1) by the latest eight checks, (2) by date, and (3) alphabetically.

The Organizer™ - 16K

This tape has two different programs. The Organizer program lets you store and retrieve information on any subject. You can organize any kind of data, such as addresses, telephone numbers, recipes, club members, customers, and so on. The computer is programmed with commands to help you search and change information in the data base you create.

The second program on this tape is called Gazetteer. It has a data base of information for every country in the world. You can find out a country's name, capital, main language(s), currency, and other information with the same commands you used with the Organizer. For example, by entering a few commands, you can easily get a list of all the Spanish-speaking countries in the world.

EDUCATIONAL

States and Capitals® - 16K

This program asks questions about the states and their capitals. You can select whether to name the state if a capital is shown, or to name the capital if a state is given.

Supermath® - 16K

Supermath has math drills on addition, subtraction, multiplication, and division. You can select one of five levels of difficulty. After ten problems, the computer shows the number of correct answers.

FINANCIAL

The Loan/Mortgage Amortizer® - 16K

This program calculates different kinds of mortgage schedules:

      1. Fixed Rate

      2. Flexible Rate

      3. Mortgage Buy—Downs

      4. Payment Schedules for Owner-Financed Items

      5. Loan Comparisons

The Stock Option Analyzer® - 16K

With this program you can analyze a possible stock option sale. Stocks are maintained with the following information you supply:

      1. Stock Symbol

      2. Strike Price

      3. Option Date

      4. Today's Date

      5. Number of Owned Shares

      6. Price Paid or Current Price

      7. Anticipated Period Dividend

8. Commission Fee
9. Number of Covered Calls
10. Call Premium
11. Commission on Writing Call

The program then calculates the return on investment (ROI), annualized ROI, net return, and last trading day.

GENERAL

Vu-Calc® - 16K

Vu-Calc calculates and displays tables of numbers and names. The user can easily change items in the table and quickly see the change's effect on a group of data. This program is an aid to financial analysis, budgets, numerical tables, statistical analysis, and other applications.

Listening to Programs

Before loading a program, be certain that you connect the earphone jack of the recorder to the earphone (EAR) jack of your computer, using one of the leads supplied.

A potential problem is that some tape recorders distort the computer's signals if the computer's microphone (MIC) and EAR leads are connected to the recorder at the same time. So, when you connect the earphone lead, do not connect the microphone lead also. As a rule, *whenever you connect the computer to a cassette recorder, do not use both the microphone and earphone leads at the same time.* Use whatever lead is needed for the task you want to do. If you want to load a cassette program into the computer, use the EAR lead. If you want to save on tape a program from the computer, use the MIC lead.

Just about any kind of cassette recorder will work with the computer. Without the EAR lead connected, adjust the volume on the tape recorder to about 3/4 of maximum. If your recorder has bass and treble controls, set the treble high and the bass low. Because computer information is high pitched, you want to emphasize high-pitched sounds.

Rewind the tape to a place before the start of the program you want to load into the computer. For a prerecorded tape with only one program, just rewind the tape all the way. If the tape has several programs, such as The Starter tape from Timex, you can rewind either to the beginning of the tape or to a place just before the beginning of the desired program. You can find that spot by rewinding and advancing the tape by trial and error until you locate where the program begins. You can identify the beginning of the program just by listening to the tape.

Let's listen to The Starter tape first so that you can learn to recognize the sound of computer signals. The programs are recorded on both sides of the tape so that you'll have a spare copy if something goes wrong. For example, you may accidentally record over a tape. You can load from either Side A or Side B. First, turn down the volume to a comfortable setting for listening.

If your recorder has an index counter, reset it to 000 and press the PLAY control. After about 10 seconds of silence you'll hear the computer signals of the program. They sound like an orchestra practicing very fast before a concert because the players are late. The label on the tape tells you that this program is the Game of Life, abbreviated as Life.

Let the tape run, and after about 15 seconds the computer sounds will stop. If you let the tape keep running, you'll hear the start of the next program, Maths. Look at the index counter on your tape recorder and subtract 3 from the index number. Make a note of this lower number as the start of Maths. Let the tape run until you hear the beginning of the third program, then note in the same way its adjusted index number.

Loading from Tape

We're ready to try the Maths program. If you have a 16K RAM Module attached to the computer, you'll have to remove the Module before loading a 2K tape. *Be sure to unplug your computer from its power source before removing or inserting the 16K RAM Module, or you may damage the RAM Module.* Rewind the tape to the adjusted index number for Maths.

Connect the EAR jack on the recorder to the EAR jack on the computer with the lead supplied. Either color will work as long as you use the same color at both ends.

Plug in your computer and adjust the TV controls so that a **K** appears as clearly as possible in the bottom left corner of the screen. If the **K** doesn't appear, remove the computer's power plug from the 9V D.C. socket and insert the plug again. Press the **J** key, and you'll see

LOAD L

appear at the bottom left corner of the screen. Notice that the **K** has disappeared and an **L** follows **LOAD**. The **K** or **L**—or some other character that may appear—act as a mark called a cursor. The *cursor* is either a white character on a black background (inverse video) or a black character on a white background (ordinary video).

Now press and hold down the red **SHIFT** key in the bottom left corner of your computer and press the **P** key. You should see a double quotation mark ('') appear because the key is shifted. Type in MATHS and then another double quotation mark. The display should look like this:

    LOAD ''MATHS'' ▉

Now, press the key labeled **ENTER**. This key sends the **LOAD** command to the computer.

If you've misspelled anything, you can correct your error simply by pulling the power cord from the 9V D.C. jack, then inserting the plug back into the jack to start over. The ▉ will appear after the computer is reset this way. If not, pull out the plug again.

Notice that the computer's memory is *volatile:* any time the computer loses power, all the memory contents are lost. If you've entered a program, have a command appearing, or have something printed on the screen, all will be lost when the power goes away. That is why it's a good idea to save a program on tape, especially when the program is long and takes much time to enter. Once the program is saved on tape, the tape retains its information even without power.

Pulling the plug is one way to correct a misspelling, particularly if you have just begun to enter information into the computer. A better way to correct a misspelling, especially if you don't want to lose what you have entered, is to move the cursor backwards character by character until you come to the place where the misspelling (or entry error) occurs, then type in the correct form of what you want to enter.

To delete backwards character by character, hold down the **SHIFT** key and press the **0** key in the upper right hand corner of the keyboard. When the **SHIFT** key is used in combination with the **0** key, the **0** key begins to function as a **DELETE** key. Every time you hold down **SHIFT** and press **DELETE**, the ▉ cursor moves backwards one step and deletes the character in that location.

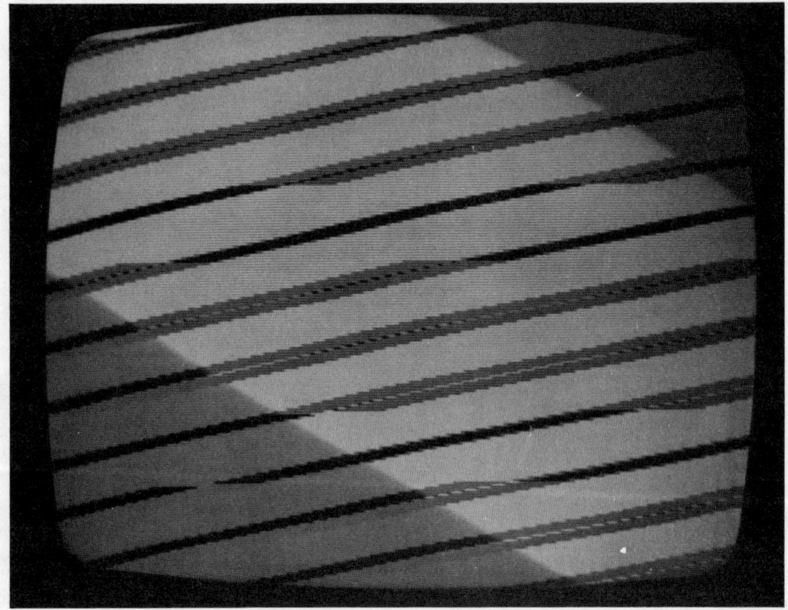

Figure 2-1
Ready for loading.

During loading, you'll first see many thin black lines slanting across the screen, as shown in Figure 2-1. This pattern indicates that the computer has accepted the command and is waiting for the program to be entered. Press the PLAY control on your recorder, and after a few seconds you'll see a different pattern (shown in Figure 2-2), which looks like thick black bars dancing up and down with the black lines we saw before. If the lines are going the opposite way, your recorder volume may be too high for the computer. Usually, however, the volume is set too low.

After about 15 seconds the bars will disappear and you should see 0/0 in the bottom left corner of the screen. This message indicates the program was successfully loaded.

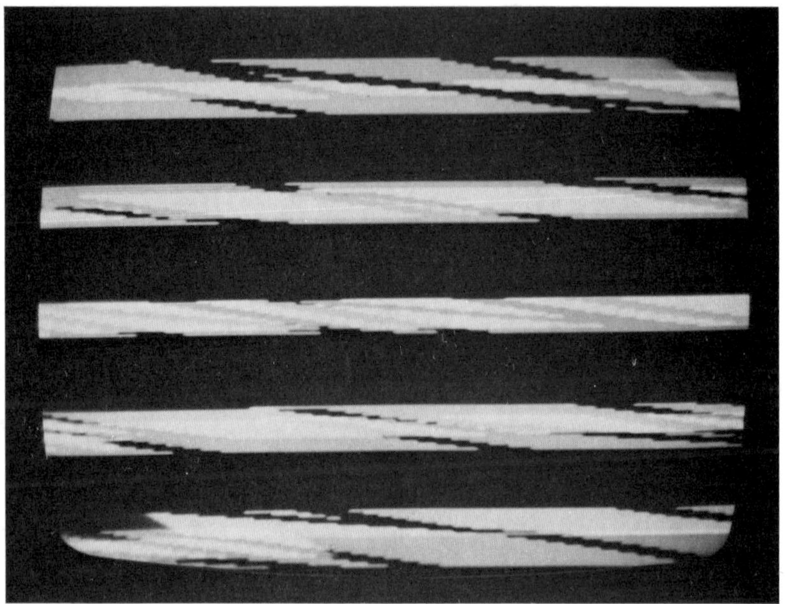

Figure 2-2
Now your program is loading.

Running the Program

Once the program is in the computer's memory, you must tell the computer to *run* the program. The computer will then execute the instructions of the program, doing whatever the program tells the computer to do.

To run the program, press the **R** key when you see the ⬚ cursor, and the word

     RUN

will appear on the screen. Notice that you didn't have to type in every letter of **R-U-N**. As mentioned earlier, your computer saves you from typing in a command letter by letter. You'll greatly appreciate this feature and similar actions if you're not a good typist. After you've programmed with the T/S 1000, you'll see how much easier it is to enter programs when you don't have to type in every letter of every word.

Now, press the **ENTER** key, and the computer will start running the program. You must *always* press the **ENTER** key after you're done typing a line. The computer won't do anything until you press **ENTER**. *From now on, we'll assume that you will press* **ENTER** *after typing a command.* On some other makes of computers, the **ENTER** key is called the **RETURN** key or **NEWLINE** key. In fact, the Maths program uses the abbreviation **N/L** for **NEWLINE**. Whenever you see **N/L**, just press the **ENTER** key. After you press the **RUN** key for Maths, you'll see

FUNCTION 1 = +; 2 = -; 3 = *; 4 = /

The "*" is the standard computer symbol for multiplication. Therefore, do not use a small "x" for multiplication, If you want multiplication drills, press the **3** key, then the **ENTER** key. For addition, press the **1** key, and so forth for the other drills.

The program then asks for a level of difficulty. If you want the hardest level, press the **3** key again.

The computer now tells you it is going to give you question number 1. You will be asked 10 questions. For each question, you can't predict what the problem will be because the computer picks each question at random. Next to the question number is shown the number of correct answers you've given so far.

Now suppose the screen shows

3*3 =

Press **9** and the computer responds

CORRECT PRESS N/L

When you press the **ENTER** key, the computer will give you another question. After 10 questions, you'll get your score. Press

ENTER again, and you'll see the menu of possible drills displayed again.

To stop the program, pull the power plug from the 9V D.C. jack, then insert the plug again. The screen should be clear, and the K should appear in the bottom left corner. If the K is not there, try again.

As mentioned earlier, when the power is removed, the contents of the computer's memory are lost. In later chapters we'll discuss other ways of stopping the program.

Once the screen is clear and the K is in the bottom left corner, you can load in another program.

Loading the Next Program

If you rewind the tape back to the beginning and enter

      LOAD "MATHS"

your computer will search the tape until it finds the first program by that name. If the tape is positioned just before the program you want loaded, you don't have to spell out the name. Just type

      LOAD""

and the computer will load into its memory the next program on the tape.

To get the "" marks, you must hold down the **SHIFT** key, then press the **P** key twice. Do not use the **Q** key! The "" marks on the **Q** key look the same to you, but not to the computer. It interprets the "" marks on the **Q** key differently.

In a later chapter, we'll discuss the use of the **Q** key. We'll also tell how to save the programs you write on tape. That way, the programs won't be lost when the power plug is pulled. You can then load in your programs from tape any time you want to use them.

CHAPTER 3
The First Steps

To do useful work, the T/S 1000 needs two things:

1. A *command*. For example, you may want it to display a number on the TV screen. The BASIC command to do this is simply **PRINT**.

2. *Data*. You've got to tell the computer what you want. The data that the computer needs is called *input*. The input can be directly supplied by you, or it can be the result of a calculation the computer has done.

Input and Output

Let's take a simple example and display a 2 on the TV screen. At the start, your display should look like this:

Now, press the key labeled **P**. Notice that above the key is the word **PRINT**. Instantly, your screen should look like this:

Notice that you didn't have to type in the whole word **P-R-I-N-T** letter by letter. The **K** is a *prompt* the computer gives you to indicate that it is expecting a *keyword* (hence, the **K**). The computer's BASIC language has a small vocabulary of these keywords, which appear above the keys of the bottom three rows of the keyboard. For example, on the bottom row the keywords are **COPY**, **CLEAR**, **CONT**, **CLS**, **SCROLL**, **NEXT**, **PAUSE**, and **BREAK**.

Whenever the **K** appears, the keyword above the key is entered after you press that key. This entry of a whole command by just one keystroke saves you much typing compared to the BASIC found on other brands of computers.

After the **PRINT** command is entered, an **L** appears. The computer now wants you to tell it what to print. The **L** stands for *literal*. That is, the T/S 1000 expects a symbol, or number, that is not a BASIC keyword the computer interprets. For example, if the **L** is present and you press the **P** key, the letter P will appear because the computer accepts the letter literally. If the **K** appeared first, the computer expects the **P** to mean the keyword **PRINT**. Press the **2** key on the top row of the keyboard. Notice that a 2 appears and the **L** moves one space to the right.

As mentioned in Chapter 2, if you accidentally typed a wrong character, you can delete it by holding the **SHIFT** key (bottom left) and then pressing the **DELETE** key (the **0** key). This combination of keystrokes deletes the character that was entered by the previous keystroke. If you need to delete more than one character to the left, just hold down the **SHIFT** key and press the delete key as many times as are necessary to remove the unwanted characters.

Suppose all you want is to have the computer print 2. You must tell the T/S 1000 you're done supplying input, and the computer should produce output using the input you've supplied. It's important to realize that the bottom line of the TV screen shows only the current input to the computer. This line just echoes what you enter. The computer actually hasn't done any useful work yet. The bottom lines are like a piece of paper for writing a message. The computer won't read your message until you say that you're done writing.

To tell the T/S 1000 you're done entering this line, just press the **ENTER** key located to the right of the ■ key.

Pressing the **ENTER** key tells the computer the input line is complete and should be entered for processing. After the **ENTER** key is pressed, the output is printed in the upper left corner of the screen, as shown below.

At the bottom left corner of the screen, some additional symbols appear. They make up a *report code* your computer displays after it processes the input. In this illustration the report code is 0/0, which means that the computer successfully accomplished the task you gave it. Notice that each zero is printed with a slash through it so that you don't confuse zero with the letter "o." It is a common practice in electronics and computer publications to print a zero as 0. The second 0 in the report code refers to the last line number the computer processed. We'll discuss line numbers in the chapter on programming. If the line number is 0, that just means you entered a command without a line number, and the computer immediately executed the command.

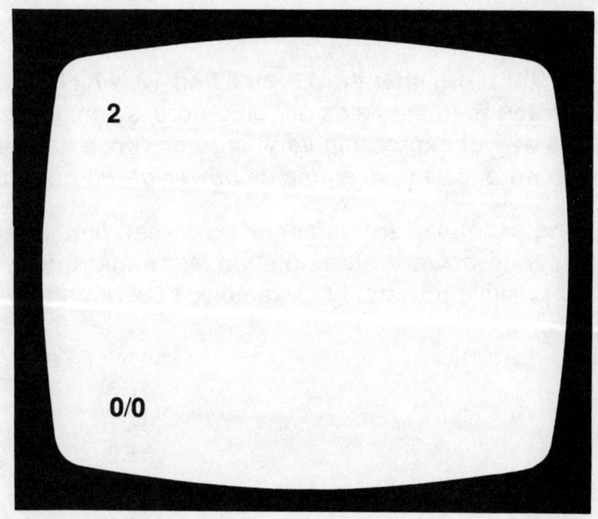

Printing Big Numbers—Power-of-Ten Notation

Now that you've gotten the hang of it, try the following:

PRINT 10

PRINT 1000

PRINT 1000000

PRINT 10000000000

PRINT 1000000000000

PRINT 10000000000000

As you can see, something unexpected happens when you try to print the last number. Instead of

    10000000000000

appearing on the screen, you get

    1E+13

If you count the zeros after the 1, you'll find 13, which is also the number after the **E**. In the fields of computers, science, and engineering, this way of expressing very large or very small numbers is common and is called *scientific* or *power-of-ten* notation.

The following examples are numbers expressed first in standard form, and then in power-of-ten notation. Note that the + sign is optional for positive powers. For example, 1E+10 can be written as 1E10.

Number	Power of Ten
1	1E0
10	1E1
100	1E2
1000	1E3
10000	1E4
12345	1.2345E4
1.5	1.5E0
2834	2.834E3

Try printing a number in power-of-ten notation from the right-hand column above, and your T/S 1000 will display the corresponding number in standard form in the left-hand column above. Use the **E** key for entering the "E."

In more general terms,

$$1E10 = 1 \times 10^{10}$$
$$1E2 = 1 \times 10^{2}$$
$$1E3 = 1 \times 10^{3}$$
$$1.2345E4 = 1.2345 \times 10^{4}$$

and so forth. The number after the "E" is called the *exponent*, and the number before the "E" is called the *mantissa*.

Now what number in standard form do you expect for the following number in power-of-ten notation?

PRINT 1E-1

Enter it and see. Note that to get a minus sign, you must first press and hold down the red **SHIFT** key at the bottom left of the keyboard. While holding down this **SHIFT**, key, press the **J** key. Notice that holding down the red **SHIFT** key calls into play the red symbols or words on the other keys. The only exceptions are the red symbols or words on the **5**, **6**, **7**, **8**, **9**, **0**, and **ENTER** keys. We'll discuss their functions in later chapters.

The result of **PRINT** 1E-1 is

0.1

because

$$1E-1 = 1 \times 10^{-1} = .1$$
$$(10^1 = 10)$$

Likewise,

$$1E-2 = 1 \times 10^{-2} = \frac{1}{10^2} = \frac{1}{100} = 0.01$$

The minus exponent means 1 divided by the number raised to the plus exponent.

Now try the following:

PRINT 1/100

Note that the division sign is on the **V** key. Also type

PRINT 1/100000

which gives .00001.

Finally, enter

PRINT 1/1000000

which gives 1E-6. If you try even smaller numbers, such as 1/10000000, you'll continue getting numbers in power-of-ten notation.

Number Limits

The largest number the computer can handle is about 1.701411E38, and the smallest number greater than 0 is 2.93873588E-39 (see *BASIC: Advanced Concepts* by J. Giarratano, published by Howard W. Sams, 1982).

For example, try

   PRINT 1.701411E38

and this number will be printed.

Now try

   PRINT 1.701412E38

and instead of the correct output, you'll see

   1.701412E38 ▓S▓

The ▓S▓ is a *syntax* error message from the computer. The message means that you're trying to do something that doesn't fit the rules of BASIC language syntax. Just like a regular language, BASIC has a vocabulary consisting of PRINT, RUN, etc., and a syntax that tells how the words can be used. In this example, the computer can't accept a number greater than 1.701411E38 and therefore flags 1.701412E38 as a syntax error.

Now try a small number like

   PRINT 2.93873588E-39

and you'll see

   2.9387359E-39

You'll get the same result for

> **PRINT** 2.93E-39
> **PRINT** 2E-39
> **PRINT** 1.9E-39
> **PRINT** 1.7E-39
> **PRINT** 1.6E-39
> **PRINT** 1.47E-39

but

> **PRINT** 1.46E-39

gives Ø.

Therefore, be careful with very small or very large numbers. Because the computer may not represent them accurately, you can get erroneous results.

CHAPTER 4
Using Your T/S 1000 as a Simple Calculator

Now that you've seen how easy it is to enter and print numbers, try using your T/S 1000 as a simple arithmetic calculator.

Addition

Suppose you want to add 2Ø + 5. Follow these steps:

Step	*Keys Pressed*	*Screen*
1.	None	

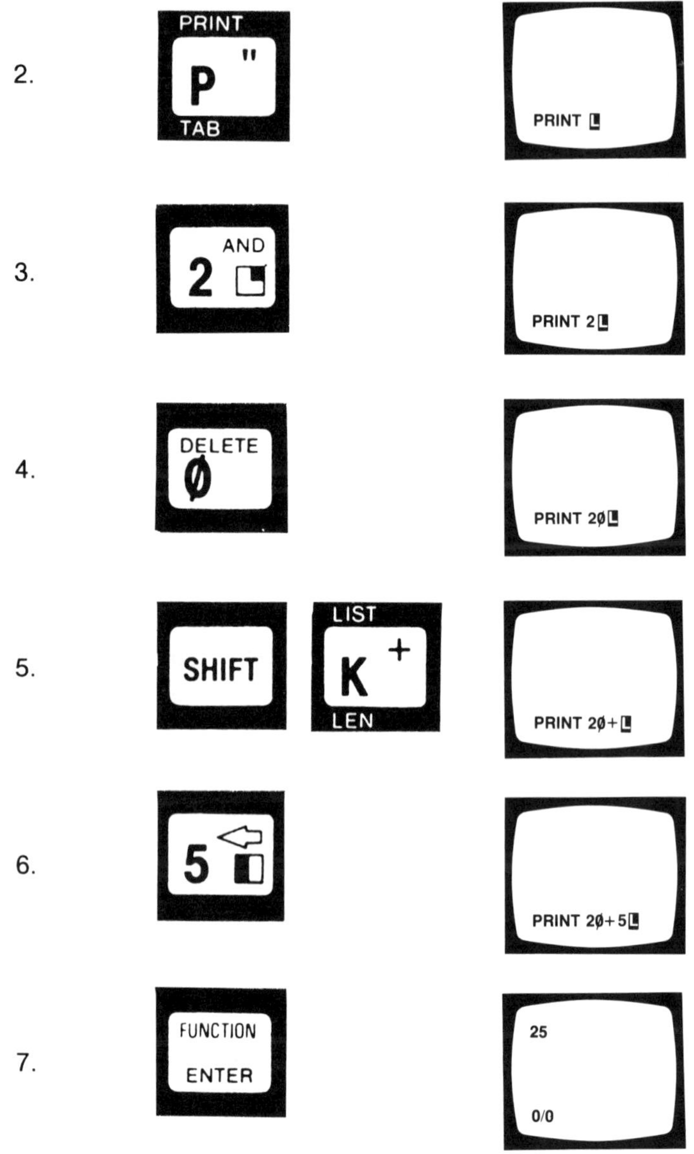

and the answer 25 appears after you press **ENTER.**

Now try

PRINT 2E-39-1E-39

The answer should be 1E-39; but because of inaccuracy with small numbers, the answer is displayed as 2.9387359E-39. Although you may never directly enter numbers as small as this, they may arise in some programs as intermediate calculations and so give errors. Therefore, never assume an answer is correct just because you use a computer.

Subtraction

Suppose you want to subtract 5 from 20. Follow the same steps 1-4, but in step 5 do the following:

5. 

Then do steps 6 and 7 as before.

Multiplication

As mentioned in Chapter 2, if you try to use "x" as the symbol for multiplication, the computer won't recognize "x." Instead, the computer uses an asterisk (*) for a multiplication sign. Therefore, in step 5, press

and do the other steps as before.

Division

For division, do the steps as before, but now use

for the division sign.

What Comes First?

Besides simple arithmetic, your T/S 1000 can also figure out more complex expressions. For example, what do you think

    PRINT 3*2 + 4

equals?

The answer is 10, because the computer first multiplies 3*2 to get 6, then adds 4 to obtain 10. Try the following:

Expression	Answer
PRINT 3*8-5	19
PRINT 4*2+8	16
PRINT 9*5+2*6	57

PRINT 3/2-2*8+1.5   -13

PRINT 7+3*5-4/2   20

The computer generally evaluates expressions from left to right. However, in the last example, the computer first multiplies 3 by 5, then stores the result internally as 15. Next, the computer divides 4 by 2 to get 2 and stores it internally. Finally, the computer adds 7 and 15, then subtracts 2 to yield 20.

The BASIC in the T/S 1000 is designed so that multiplication and division occur before addition and subtraction. Otherwise, in that last example, the computer would have first added 7 and 3 to get 10, then multiplied it by 5 to get 50, subtracted 4 to get 46, then divided this by 2 to get 23. If all operators had equal priority, the answer would have been 23 instead of 20.

BASIC is designed to have the kind of operator priority that most people are familiar with. That is why multiplication and division come before addition and subtraction. Between multiplication and division, the two are treated equally. For example, try

Example	*Answer*
PRINT 4*8/16	2
PRINT 8/16*4	2

Notice that if multiplication had higher priority than division, the answer above would have been

8/(16*4)

=8/64

=0.125

instead of 2. Of course, you can always use parentheses to force the arithmetic priority in the order you want. For example,

PRINT 8/(16*4)

=0.125.

Likewise, addition and subtraction have no precedence between themselves. To illustrate, try the following:

PRINT 8+4-2

PRINT 4-2+8

Both give 1Ø as the answer.

A Special Case of the Minus Sign

As with most rules, there is at least one exception. What do you think

PRINT 3*-2

will give?

The computer will answer -6, because 3 times -2 is -6. Notice that we don't want to subtract 2 from 3. In fact, the computer wouldn't even accept this as subtraction because of the * after the 3. We want the minus sign in front of the 2 to be interpreted as the number -2.

When the minus sign is used to negate (make negative) the following, it's called a *unary minus.* For example, **PRINT** -2 prints a - 2 on the screen, because we negated a plus 2. And **PRINT** --2 prints 2 because we negated a minus 2. The term "unary," which comes from Latin and means "one," is fitting because it applies to the *one* thing that follows it.

However, in the case of 4-2, the minus is called *binary minus* after the Latin word "binary," which means "two." In this illustration, the binary minus relates *two* numbers: the 4 and the 2. Therefore, a unary operation applies to one number, but a binary operator applies to two.

Try these other examples of unary minus and notice how they differ from a binary minus operation.

Example	Answer
PRINT -2*3	-6
PRINT 8*-3+3	-21
PRINT -2*3+8	2

PRINT -2*-2*-2-2	-10
PRINT -10/-2*-5-2	-27

In particular, notice how this last example is calculated. The computer divides -10 by -2 to get 5, multiplies this by -5 to get -25, then subtracts 2 to get -27. The unary minus has higher priority than multiplication or division. This priority means that in evaluating any expression the computer

1. does any unary minus operations,
2. then multiplies and divides,
3. and then adds and subtracts.

All of these operations are done from left to right.

Parentheses

If you're in doubt about how something will be evaluated, you can always use parentheses to force the evaluation the way you want. Notice that the left parenthesis is on the **I** key and the right parenthesis on the **O** key. For example, try the following:

PRINT -10/(-2*-5-2)

It gives -1.25 because the expression in parentheses is evaluated as follows. First the unary minus is applied to make a -2 and a -5, then the expression is evaluated:

$$=-10/((-2*-5)-2)$$
$$=-10/(10-2)$$
$$=-10/8$$
$$=-1.25$$

Actually, you are already used to doing arithmetic like this. It's just something that most people don't even think about when they do arithmetic. Try practicing with some expressions, and you'll see how easily the computer evaluates expressions for you.

CHAPTER 5
Printing

Besides printing numbers, your computer can also print individual characters or strings of characters. For example, try

PRINT "JOE"

where you get " by using the **SHIFT** key with the **P** key. You can print anything between the quotation marks, even numerals. Try

PRINT "1Ø14 MAIN STREET"

For a space, use the **SPACE** key at the bottom right of the keyboard. All the characters between quotation marks are a *string of characters,* which is commonly called a *string.* Characters can be any printable symbol, even $<$, $<>$, $>$, ., etc.

Another interesting feature is *adding characters.* What do you get when you add apples and oranges? Try this and see:

PRINT "APPLES" + "ORANGES"

The answer is APPLESORANGES since the + operator combines strings in the order they're given. This combining of strings is called *concatenation* and is useful in certain programs.

If you try any other arithmetic operator, such as *, /, or -, you'll just get a syntax error message, because only the + is allowed in this BASIC.

The keyboard of your computer is a real marvel of efficient design. Besides the standard alphabetic characters and numerals, you can also print *graphics symbols* and *inverse video characters*. The graphics symbols or characters are the small squares on some keys in the upper three rows of the keyboard. These symbols can be printed on your screen. Of course, the resolutions of different TVs may make some characters harder to read.

For example, to print the graphics character on a key,

> (1) press and hold down the red **SHIFT** key,

> (2) then press **9**, the **GRAPHICS** key. You'll see the cursor change to a **G**, showing you're in graphics mode.

> (3) While still holding down the **SHIFT** key, press the **E** key—or any key with a small square graphics symbol in the lower right corner. That symbol will be printed on the screen. You have to hold down the **SHIFT** key because the graphics symbol is a shifted key.

To get an inverse video symbol, follow steps (1) and (2) above. Now release the **SHIFT** key. Press any key, and the inverse video, *unshifted* version will appear. For example, press the **E** key, and you'll see a white E on a black background. Also, the period appears white on a black background, and the **SPACE** key just gives a black square.

Printing Quotations

An interesting question arises in printing strings. How do you print quotations? Because everything between quotation marks is printed, you can't include just quotations. Try entering the following:

> **PRINT** ""HELLO""

You'll just get a syntax error message.

To avoid this problem, use a special set of quotation marks that is provided. This set is called the *quote image* and is located on the **Q** key as a shifted character. Just press the **SHIFT** key and **Q** to obtain the quote image. Try this:

1. Press **P** to get **PRINT**
2. Press the **P** key to get "
3. Press the **Q** key to get ""
4. Spell out HELLO
5. Press the **Q** key to get ""
6. Press the **P** key to get "

and you should see

PRINT """"HELLO""""

where the "" before the H and after the O begin and end the quote image. Now press **ENTER** and you'll see

"HELLO"

at the top of the screen. Notice that HELLO is in quotation marks now. If you just do a

PRINT "HELLO"

you'll see

HELLO

without quotation marks.

Printing Strings and Numbers

It's handy to be able to combine strings and numbers. For example, try entering the following:

PRINT "ANSWER=",2+2

and you'll see

ANSWER=   4

where 9 blank spaces appear between the 4 and the = sign. Now try

    PRINT "ANSWER=";2+2

and you'll see

    ANSWER=4

The semicolon after the second quotation mark tells the computer to print the 4 just after the = sign. When the comma was used in the first example, the 4 was printed at the 17th column from the left. To see the position of the 4 more clearly, enter

    PRINT "123456789012345",2+2

and you'll see

    123456789012345 4

The capability of printing strings and numbers can greatly improve the readability of your output.

Controlling Printing by Using Commas

Now try

    PRINT "1234567890123456",2+2

and you'll see

    1234567890123456
    4

What happened? This version of BASIC is designed to move the printing position one space from the last character printed, then print the next item. Therefore, in this illustration, the printing position after the last 6, which is in column 16, is column 17. Another principle is that a comma forces printing to start at either the 1st or 17th column—whichever next follows the comma. The comma functions much like a tab key on a typewriter, moving the printhead to a specified location. Now in the illustration above, the comma in the 17th column directs printing to the 1st column of the next line. Thus, the comma forces the printing of 4, the sum of 2 + 2, to start in the 1st column of the next line.

In short, if an item can't be printed in the 17th column (because a comma is there, pointing to the 1st column of the next line), the item is printed in the 1st column of the next line (unless a comma is there also, pointing to the 17th column). Try the following:

Example	*Answer*	
	Col 1	Col 17
PRINT ,1	—(16 spaces)—	1
PRINT 1,1	1—(15 spaces)—	1
PRINT 1,1,1	1—(15 spaces)—	1
	1	
PRINT 1,,1	1	
	1	
PRINT 1,,,1	1	
	—(16 spaces)—	1
PRINT 1,,,,1	1	
	(one blank line)	
	1	

As you can see from these examples, each comma forces printing to start at either the 1st or 17th column. If the 17th column is not available, printing starts at the 1st column on a new line, unless forced past by another comma.

Where It's "AT"

You can also control the printing position with another BASIC command. Try

PRINT AT 0,0;"1"

To print the **AT** keyword, you must press **"SHIFT"** and the **"FUNCTION"** key and you'll see the computer █ prompt change to the *function* prompt, █ . Now press the **C** key, which has the word **AT** below it. This procedure is the general way to access functions printed below a key. After you enter this **PRINT** line, a **1** will appear in the upper left corner of the screen. Now try

      PRINT AT 0,31;1   (prints at top right)
      PRINT AT 21,0;1   (prints at bottom left)
      PRINT AT 21,31;1   (prints at bottom right)
      PRINT AT 11,16;1   (prints about the middle of
                                       screen)

For use with the **PRINT AT** command, the screen is divided into 22 rows and 32 columns, as shown in Figure 5-1. The rows are numbered from 0 to 21 from the top down; and the columns, from 0 to 31 from left to right. The first number after **AT** is the row number, and the second number is the column number. The correct form of the statement is seen in the following:

      PRINT AT row,column;item

where the item can be either a number or a string. For example, try

      PRINT AT 5,5,"HELLO"

The **AT** command allows you to print anywhere on the top 22 lines of the screen and use any symbol. You can print inverse video characters and graphics symbols with **PRINT AT** or **PRINT**. However, **PRINT** always prints below the last printed line. **PRINT AT** gives you control over where items are printed. If you exceed the allowed printing positions on the screen, you'll get a report code of B. For example, try

PRINT AT 35,Ø;"HELLO"

If you look up this report code in Appendix C, it says "integer out of range." The reason is that 35 in the **PRINT AT** statement is greater than the allowed range of Ø to 21.

Tabs

Just as you can control printing with the tab key on a typewriter, you can use the **TAB** command to control printing with the computer. As is true for the **AT** command, you access **TAB** by pressing **SHIFT** and **FUNCTION**, then the **P** key. Also, just like **AT**, columns are numbered from Ø to 31. Try the following:

PRINT TAB 1Ø; "HELLO"

and HELLO appears near the middle of the top line of the screen. Now try

PRINT TAB 31; "HELLO"

As you can see, the H is printed in column 31, but ELLO appears on the next line.

Clearing the Screen

If you ever get a report code of 5, that means the screen is full. No more printing or execution can occur until the screen is cleared. Also, you may want to clear the screen even before it's full. To clear the screen, just press the **CLS** key, which is the **V** key. For example, input

PRINT 1ØØ

and you'll see a 1ØØ printed in the top left.

Now press the **V** key, and you'll see **CLS** appear on the bottom line:

CLS

Press **ENTER**, and the **CLS** command will clear the screen. Only a 0/0 report will remain.

Try practicing more examples of these operations. The more you use the keyboard, the less time it will take you to find the symbol you're looking for. Like any other skill, learning how to use the computer just takes practice—and patience.

CHAPTER 6
Using the T/S 1000 As a Supercalculator

Your T/S 1000 has many math functions not found in a simple calculator. These functions are convenient to have when you write computer programs or just use the T/S 1000 as a supercalculator for school, work, or personal use.

PI

PI is the math function (π) = 3.141592..., which is the ratio of the circumference of a circle to its diameter. The value for PI stored in your computer is an approximation to the true value, which cannot be specified exactly by a finite number of digits. That is why we've put dots after the value of PI above.

The symbol for PI is located under the **M** key and is accessed as a *function* key.

First, be sure you see the **K** cursor. Now press **P** and the word **PRINT** will appear. To get PI, you've got to

1. hold down **SHIFT**, then press the **ENTER** key. You'll see the cursor change from ▊ to ▊ . This change means the computer is ready to print a math function under the keys.

2. Next, press the **M** key and you'll see

PRINT PI ▊

on the screen. Notice that PI appears instead of the symbol π.

Now press the **ENTER** key, and the computer will print the value of PI:

	Answer
PRINT PI	3.1415927

You can access any of the functions under the keys by following steps (1) and (2). We'll refer to functions under the keys from now on as *shifted functions.*

As an example, the circumference of a circle 1Ø feet in diameter is PI * Diameter:

	Answer
PRINT PI*1Ø	31.415927

The area of a circle with a 5-foot radius is PI * Radius^2:

	Answer
PRINT PI*5*5	78.539816

The volume of a sphere = 4/3 PI * Radius^3.

Therefore, for a 1Ø-foot radius, enter:

	Answer
PRINT 4***PI***1Ø*1Ø*1Ø/3	4188.79Ø2

PI is stored in the computer with greater accuracy than the 8 digits printed by the **PRINT** command. To show the extra digits, try

	Answer
PRINT PI-3.141	.00059265364

Therefore, PI is stored as about 3.14159265364.

Powers

In the volume calculation earlier, you had to enter

10*10*10

Instead of entering each factor individually, you can use *powers* since

$$10*10*10 = 10^3$$

The power function is labeled as ****** on the **H** key. Just hold down **SHIFT**, then press **H** to access this function. Now try

PRINT 4*PI*10**3/3

and you'll get the same answer as before.

The power function is convenient because it's so general. For example, what's the 4/5 power of 13? Try

	Answer
PRINT 13**(4/5)	7.7831371

Notice that the parentheses are necessary, or else we evaluate

$$13^4/5$$

which is not the same.

The reason is that powers have higher precedence than multiplication and division. Appendix B shows the priority of the functions and operations. Although we haven't discussed all of them yet, you can see the priority of those we have. The priority number is a relative value showing which functions and operations have priority over others. The ones with higher priority are evaluated before the ones with lower priority.

Now try

PRINT 13**4/5

and see how different the answer is. You can also use decimal powers. For example,

	Answer
PRINT 16**.5	4

since the .5 power is the square root:

$$16^{.5} = \sqrt{16}$$

Square Root

Square root is also given as a math function, which appears under the **H** key as **SQR**. Try

	Answer
PRINT SQR 16	4
PRINT SQR 625	25

Approximations and Precision

The calculations done by the computer with powers and other math functions are generally correct. However, small errors may creep into the calculations because the computer calculates and stores numbers to only a certain degree of precision. For example, the square root of 16 is 4. If we subtract 4, we should get Ø. But do we? Try

	Answer
PRINT 16**.5-4	-1.8626452E-9

which is not zero. But if you use the **SQR** function, you do get the correct answer of Ø.

	Answer
PRINT SQR 16-4	Ø

The computer displays an answer of 4 for either

PRINT 16**.5

or

PRINT SQR 16

but, as you can see, the square root calculated by the function ** is slightly less than 4 by 1.8626452E-9. The **PRINT** command rounds off the result to 4 because this difference is minute. However, if the true value of 4 is subtracted from the square root, the difference shows up. Therefore, what you see displayed is not necessarily what you get.

When square root is calculated by the **SQR** function, the computer uses a different technique, or algorithm. An *algorithm* is a method of solving a problem. In fact, any computer program is an algorithm expressed in a specific computer language. The same algorithm can be expressed in different languages, such as FOR-TRAN, COBOL, or Pascal, and give the same result.

The algorithm for calculating the **SQR** function is more exact than the general algorithm for powers.

Again, this illustration shows that the computer is not perfect. As is true for any computer, you must keep in mind its limitations as you work with it. People who know nothing about computers may assume that all their answers are perfectly correct. However, the computer is just a tool; and, like any tool, it has limitations. As you work with the computer, you'll see what these limitations are and how you can compensate for them.

Integer Function

The integer function rounds down a number to the next smallest integer. It's a shifted function located under the **R** key. Try

	Answer
PRINT INT 2.1	2
PRINT INT 10.9	10
PRINT INT 2.5	2
PRINT INT (2.5 + .5)	3

Notice that by adding .5 to 2.5 we have rounded the number 2.5 up to 3. In general, you can round up by adding .5 to any number. Now try

	Answer
PRINT INT -2.1	-3

This answer may seem surprising until you realize that -3 is less than -2.1. Since -3 is less than -2.1, the computer rounds down to -3. If you want to round any number up to the next highest integer, just add .5 first. For example

	Answer
PRINT INT (-2.1 + .5)	-2
PRINT INT (5.1 + .5)	5
PRINT INT (5.5 + .5)	6

You can see that the **INT** function does round off numbers. It does not just truncate, or cut off, their decimal part.

Dollars and Cents

An important application of the **INT** function is with numbers that have decimal parts. Try the following:

	Answers
PRINT 10-1	10
PRINT 10.1-.1	10
PRINT 100.15-.05	100.1
PRINT 18.23-.01	18.22

The numbers above all work out as you expect them to. Now try

	Answer
PRINT 64.1-64	.099999994

The answer is in error because, as indicated earlier, numbers are held only to a certain degree of precision in the computer. This problem may appear when you use numbers with decimal parts, called *floating point numbers*. Some floating point numbers cause more trouble then others. Those that do are usually numbers with a decimal part of .1.

It's a particular problem if you want to write a program for financial applications. However, there is an easy solution. Just round off the answer.

To round off any number N to two decimal places, use

INT (100*N + .5)/1000

For example, try

	Answer
PRINT INT (100*1 + .5)/100	1
PRINT INT (100*1.5 + .5)/100	1.5
PRINT INT (100*1.555 + .5)/100	1.56
PRINT INT (100*23.8947 + .5)/100	23.89
PRINT INT (100*.(64.1-64) + .5)/100	.1

If you want to round off to three decimal places, use **1000** instead of **100**, and so forth.

Exponential Function

The exponential function gives the powers relative to the base of natural logarithms; e = 2.7182818....

Like PI, base "e" can't be written exactly with a finite number of digits. On the keyboard, "e" is labeled as the shifted function **EXP** under the **X** key.

In general, EXP N = e^N, where N is any number. Try

	Answer
PRINT EXP 1	2.7182818
PRINT EXP 2.5	12.182494

Natural Logarithm

The natural log, the inverse function of **EXP**, is the shifted function **LN** under the **Z** key. In general, X = **LN(EXP** X), and that is why **LN** and **EXP** are called inverse functions. You can get back the number you started with, X, by using the inverse function:

$$X = \textbf{EXP}(\textbf{LN}\ X)$$

Try

	Answer
PRINT LN 1	0
PRINT LN 2.7182818	0.99999999

Notice that you didn't get back 1 exactly. Now try

	Answer
PRINT LN EXP 1	1

The answer is 1. It may seem odd that when you used **LN** 2.7182818, the answer was wrong. But, **LN EXP** 1 turns out all right. The reason why this happens is that the computer calculates **EXP** 1 more accurately than what it displays by the **PRINT** command. This problem is the same one we saw before, where **PRINT** 16**.5 gave 4, but the difference 16**.5-4 was not 0.

You're using a more accurate number in

    PRINT LN EXP 1

than in

    PRINT LN 2.7182818

To show more decimal places, remove the leading digit by subtracting 2. Try

	Answer
PRINT EXP 1-2	.71828183

Notice that now an extra significant digit of .00000003 appears. To prove that this is a better approximation, try

	Answer
PRINT LN 2.71828183	1

Now the answer is printed as 1. Also try

PRINT 2.71828183

This is printed on your screen as 2.7182818, but the computer stores it with the 2.71828183, since

PRINT LN 2.71828183

gives 1, and

PRINT LN 2.7182818

gives 1.02345641.

Although the **LN** function is convenient for certain kinds of calculations, most people are used to logs to base 10. To convert any **LN** to base 10, just divide by **LN** 10. For example,

	Answer
PRINT LN 2/**LN** 10	.30103
PRINT LN 3/**LN** 10	.47712126
PRINT LN 100/**LN** 10	2

Absolute Value Function

The absolute value function, **ABS**, always returns the positive value of a number. If the number is positive, it is returned. If the number is negative, then the negative of it (a positive) is returned. The absolute function key, **ABS**, is a shifted function under the **G** key. Try

	Answer
PRINT ABS 5	5
PRINT ABS -5	5
PRINT ABS (2*3+1)	7

Sign Function

The sign function, **SGN**, is a shifted function key under the **F** key and returns a +1 if a number is positive, 0 if the number is 0, and -1 if the number is negative. Try

	Answer
PRINT SGN 5	1
PRINT SGN Ø	Ø
PRINT SGN -5	-1
PRINT SGN (2*3+1)	1

Random Function

The random function, **RND**, gives a number greater than, or equal to, Ø, and less than 1. **RND** is not a true random number generator, but instead picks one out of a sequence of 65,536 numbers that are almost random. **RND** is a shifted function under the **T** key. Try

    PRINT RND

    PRINT RND

    PRINT RND

RND is called a *pseudorandom* generator (pseudo means false) because it acts like a true random number generator, but really isn't. The 65,536 numbers follow a certain order that doesn't change. The **RND** function just gets a number from somewhere in the sequence. To get always the same sequence, use the **RAND** keyword followed by a number between 1 and 65,535. With **RAND**, you can always start off **RND** at a specific place in the pseudorandom sequence. **RAND** is a keyword above the **T** key. To access **RAND**, be sure you have a ⓚ, then press the **T** key. The **RAND** will appear.

For example, try

	Answer
RAND 5	
PRINT RND	.ØØ68511963
PRINT RND	Ø.51496887
RAND 5	
PRINT RND	.ØØ68511963
PRINT RND	Ø.51496887
RAND 5	

| **PRINT RND** | .0068511963 |
| **PRINT RND** | 0.51496887 |

The same numbers are given each time for **RND**. The number following **RAND** can range from 1 to 65,535. However, if you use **RAND 0**, you'll get different numbers each time. The **RAND 0** picks a number in the sequence based on the number of TV frames that have been shown so far on the TV up to a maximum value. The TV picture is actually a succession of still pictures displayed 60 times a second. Every two frames make up a single still picture.

Trig Functions

Figure 6-1 shows the fundamental trig functions for a right triangle. The angle **T** must be expressed in radians, not degrees, for the computer's trig functions. Radians are a common measure of angles in science and engineering. Fig. 6-2 shows an arc of a circle of radius 1. If the arc subtended by the angle is of length 1, then the angle T is 1 radian. One radian is about 57.3°. Since the circumference of a circle is 2*PI*radius, then there are 2*PI radians in a circle, or 2*PI radians = 360°.

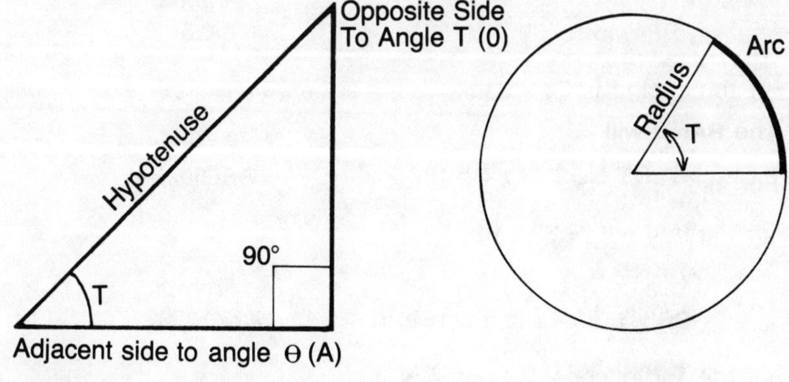

Figure 6-1   *Figure 6-2*

Since 2*PI radians = 360°, then

$$1° = 2*PI/360 = PI/180 \text{ radians}$$

For example, the radians equivalent of 30° is

	Answer
PRINT 30***PI**/180	0.52359878 radians

and the degree equivalent of 0.52359878 radians is

	Answer
PRINT 0.52359878*180/**PI**	30°

Trig Function	*Computer Function Equivalent for Angle T in Radians*
SINE (T) = O/H	**SIN** T
COSINE (T) = A/H	**COS** T
TANGENT (T) = O	**TAN** T
ARCSINE (O/H) = T	**ARCSIN** O/H
ARCCOS (A/H) = T	**ARCCOS** A/H
ARCTAN (O/A) = T	**ARCTAN** O/H

Suppose you want the sine of 30°. Then you want to

	Answer
PRINT SIN (30***PI**/180)	0.5

For the cosine of 30°, use

	Answer
PRINT COS (30***PI**/180)	0.8660254

For the tangent of 30°, use

	Answer
PRINT TAN (30***PI**/180)	0.57735027

For the angle whose sine is 0.5, use

	Answer
PRINT ASN (0.5)	0.52359878

Notice that the arcsin is printed as **ASN** by the computer. An answer of Ø.52359878 is returned for the arcsin of Ø.5. You can check to see if this corresponds to 30° by

	Answer
PRINT 30*PI/180	Ø.52359878

and in fact **PRINT SIN** .52359878 does give Ø.5.

CHAPTER 7
BASIC Programming

The real difference between a computer and a calculator is that the computer can perform calculations automatically—that is, the computer can carry out a series of instructions without your having to enter them manually each time. The computer stores the instructions in its memory. Then, when you enter data, the computer follows those instructions one step at a time to process the data. A general term for computer instructions is *software,* in contrast to the computer's hardware or physical components.

Line Numbers and Memory

The instructions for the computer are stored as numbered lines, called *statements,* in its memory. The computer executes, or performs, each statement in order, beginning with the lowest line number and proceeding to the next higher line number. A group of lines that performs a task is a *program.* Sometimes programs are broken down into smaller groups, called *modules.* Each module performs a single function. This simplifies the task of writing a program because it can be broken down into smaller portions that are easy to write and test independently. As an example of a simple program, enter

    10 **RAND** 5
    20 **PRINT RND**
    30 **PRINT RND**

Just type in the line number, then the command, such as **RAND** or **PRINT RND**, for each line of the program. You can use any line numbers as long as they are integers from 1 to 9999 and increase in the ascending order shown. Notice that you don't have to put any spaces after the line numbers or commands. Your T/S 1000 has a smart BASIC language that helps you to write legible programs.

Once you see the ▓ cursor, you only have to press the keyword **RUN**, then **ENTER**, to execute this program. The label **RUN** is easy to find above the **R** key. Several of the BASIC commands are similarly located above a key whose letter is the first letter of the command.

When you press **RUN** (and **ENTER**), you'll see the same results for random numbers that we got in the section on Random Numbers in Chapter 6. Press **RUN** again, and the same numbers will appear. In fact, every time you press **RUN**, the same numbers always appear because we're using the same **RAND** 5.

As mentioned earlier, unless it is instructed otherwise, the computer executes first the lowest line number of your program— 10 in this illustration; then, the next highest, 20; and so on. The program lines are stored in the computer's memory. The standard T/S 1000 comes with 2K bytes of memory, where K = 1024, giving a total of 2048 bytes. A *byte* is a unit of memory capacity and can contain one character of data: a letter of the alphabet, a numeral, a symbol, or a code that represents a keyword or function, such as **PRINT** and **EXP**.

Actually, not all the 2K bytes are available for your use. Some are used by BASIC, and others are used for the TV display. Bigger programs with more lines use more memory. If you keep running out of memory, you may wish to buy some additional memory, such as the 16K RAM Module.

After you've run the program, take a look at the report code at the bottom of the screen. Notice that it's no longer Ø/Ø, which appeared for the commands executed without a line number. The first character is the report code, which provides information. Depending on the code, it may be an error report or just a status report. For example, you get a report code of 6 if you try to divide a number by Ø. However, a report code of 5 is just a status report, meaning the screen is full of data, and the computer doesn't want to execute any more of the program until you say it's okay to continue. If you look at Appendix C, you'll see that a Ø report code means successful completion. The second number shows the last line that was executed. Commands executed without a line number are always assigned a Ø.

Listing Programs

Anytime the computer is not executing, you can see your program by using the **LIST** command, located above the **K** key. Press **LIST** (and **ENTER**), and you'll see the program stored in the computer's memory.

Should you have a Timex/Sinclair printer attached to your computer, the **COPY** command, located above the **Z** key, will print out everything on the screen. An **LLIST** command will *list* the program on the printer. An **LPRINT** command will *print* the output on the printer.

Now enter

    LIST 3Ø

Notice that only line 3Ø appears on the screen. Now try

    LIST 2Ø

Lines 2Ø and 3Ø are on the screen. The **LIST** command starts listing your program from whatever line is given to the end of the program, if possible. If you use the **LIST** command without a line number, the listing will show in sequence the line numbers greater than 0.

As you keep entering lines in your program, an interesting thing happens. Enter

> 10 **PRINT**
>
> 20 **PRINT**
>
> 30 **PRINT**

and so on all the way to

> 220 **PRINT**

Be sure to enter **PRINT** statements from 40 to 210.

Now enter

> 230 **PRINT**

Where is line 10? It has left the screen to make way for line 230, but it is still stored in memory. To check this, do a **LIST**.

Now enter

> 240 **PRINT**
>
> 250 **PRINT**

You will see lines 40 to 250, because the screen can only show 22 lines at a time. If your program is longer than 22 lines, you will have to list it in stages. In this case, you would enter

> **LIST**

and then

> **LIST** 230

to show the rest of the program.

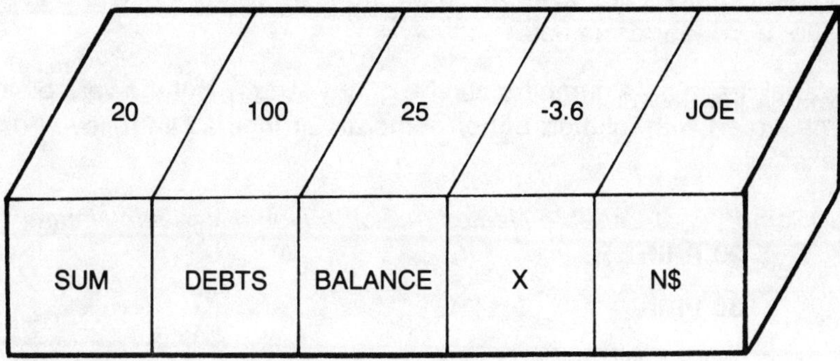

Figure 7-1
Box concept of variable storage.

Variables

One feature that has made the computer such a powerful and useful tool is the *variable*—a storage area in the computer's memory for numbers or characters.

Figure 7-1 illustrates this concept as a box with its contents. For example, the number 20 was put in the variable SUM; 100 was put in DEBTS, 25 in BALANCE, -3.6 in X, and the string of characters "JOE" was put in N$. Notice that variables to hold strings must have only a single letter name and must be followed by a $ sign. These are called *string variables* because they can contain a string of characters. The characters can be any symbols, such as letters, numerals, graphics symbols, punctuation marks, etc.

Each character of a variable name uses one byte of memory. Therefore, if you don't have much memory capacity, you should keep variable names short. For example, you could use S instead of SUM, as a variable name. The only drawback to using short names or single letters is that it is harder for a person to read a program and understand what it is doing. On the other hand, the computer takes longer and executes more slowly when longer variable names are used. As a compromise, you can use abbreviations for longer names.

Variables to hold numbers can be of any length, but the variables must start with a letter. Either numerals or letters can follow. For example:

Some Legal Variable Names	*Some Illegal Variable Names*
DEBTS	IX
A	< >
X	¡A
B1	A?
XYZ12345	WXY)
MORTGAGE	N1$
POINTS	
COMMISSION	
GRADES	

Variables that hold numbers are called *numeric variables.*

Assigning Numbers or Strings to Variables

You can assign a number or a string to a variable by using the keyword **LET**, located above the **L** key and followed by an equal sign. The equal sign is a shifted **L** key. Try the following simple program:

    10 **LET** NUMBER=5

    20 **PRINT** NUMBER

Line 10 defines a numeric variable called NUMBER and puts a 5 in it. Run this program, and the number 5 will appear at the top of your screen. Try making up your own variable names and running this program with different numbers assigned to it. Notice that since the program above worked, the report code is Ø, and the last line executed was 20.

Now enter and run the following program:

    10 **LET** X=25

```
20 LET Y=10
30 LET SUM=X+Y
40 PRINT "SUM=";SUM
50 LET A$="DONE"
60 PRINT A$
```

At the top of the screen, you will see

```
SUM=35
DONE
```

We have combined the string "SUM=" and the numeric variable SUM in line 40 to print an informative message.

Another way to get the same message is to assign "SUM" to a string variable and print that. For example, use

```
25 LET S$="SUM="
40 PRINT S$;SUM
```

and you'll get the same results.

Also, notice how line 25 is automatically inserted by the computer between lines 20 and 30.

Now you can see why it is a good idea to number your original program lines in increments of 10. You can then insert up to 9 lines after each of your original instruction lines if you wish. Note, too, that there is no relation between the string "SUM" and the variable SUM.

Suppose you decide to modify the program so that it will change the value of SUM by a factor of 1.9 before printing it. One way this can be done is by adding the line

```
35 LET SUM=1.9*SUM
```

and running the program again.

There is an even simpler way to write the original program. If you don't need the variable SUM for anything else, you can replace it as follows:

```
10 LET X=25
20 LET Y=10
30 PRINT "SUM=";X+Y
40 PRINT "DONE"
```

Eliminating unnecessary variables saves memory space and increases execution speed.

Editing Programs

To delete a line from a program, just type the line number and press the **ENTER** key. To change a line, you can either

1. retype the line with corrections. For example, type in

   30 PRINT "DIFFERENCE=";X-Y

   and press the **ENTER** key. This new line will replace the old line 30, or

2. use the **EDIT** key, the number **1** key shifted. An arrow ' points to the first command of the line you just entered.

   30 ▶ PRINT "DIFFERENCE=";X-Y

This arrow is a cursor. You can move it to any line you want to edit by using the arrows on keys **6** and **7**. Simply hold down the **SHIFT** key and press the arrow marking the direction in which you want to go. The cursor will move in the direction of the arrow on the key each time you press it. For example, if the cursor is on line 30, and you want to move the cursor to line 10, hold down **SHIFT** and press the up arrow key (**7**). Each time you press **7**, the cursor will move up a line.

When the cursor is on the line you want to edit, hold down **SHIFT** and then press the **EDIT** key (**1**). The line will appear at the bottom of the screen. The top 22 lines of the display are reserved for programs, but the bottom line is for editing and entering lines. As the edited line gets longer, part of the program's top lines may be moved off the display. Normally, 32 characters can fit on a line.

After you move to line 10 and use the **EDIT** key, you'll notice that there is a **K** in front of the **LET** command. The **K** shows that a keyword is expected next. Now that you are editing a line, you can move the cursor either right or left by using the arrows on keys **5** and **8**. Hold down **SHIFT** and tap the right arrow once. The cursor will jump past **LET** and change to an **L** to show that literals are now expected.

Press the left arrow on key **5,** and the cursor will jump back across **LET.** Now press the right arrow twice to move the cursor just past the X. Next, press the **R** key, and the letter R will be added to make XR. To delete the R, hold **SHIFT** and press **DELETE.** When you are satisfied with the line, press **ENTER,** and the new line will replace the one in memory. You can even edit a line number. Move the cursor just to the right of the line number and delete it. Then enter 25 as the new line. Press **ENTER,** and the edited line will flash back on the screen. Notice that you now have a

      10 **LET** X = 25

and a

      25 **LET** X = 25

By changing the line number, you made a duplicate of the contents.

Suppose you have a long program and want to edit a line far from the cursor. You can easily move the cursor near that line without having to press the arrow key a number of times. For example, move the cursor down to line 40. Now suppose you want to edit line 20. Enter

      15 **PRINT**

into your program.

Line 15 will appear with the cursor just above line 20. Now delete line 15 by entering the number 15 **ENTER**. You can include any command in the line to be deleted, because this statement is being entered only to move the cursor. The whole idea is to enter a line, then delete it to reset the cursor to the following line.

Although the cursor has disappeared from the screen, the computer knows where it is. Press **SHIFT** and **EDIT**. Line 20 will appear on the bottom of the screen, waiting to be edited.

Another way is to **LIST** the line number you want. For example, move the cursor back to line 10. Now enter

    LIST 40

and the cursor will appear on line 40. Notice, too, that the listed line is now at the top of the screen.

Continuing Printing

The use of **PRINT** in a program statement allows more flexibility than a simple **PRINT** command. Try

    10 **PRINT** 3,

    20 **PRINT** 30

The output appears as though the single command **PRINT** 3,30 had been entered. A comma at the end of a line forces the next **PRINT** output to either the 1st or the 17th column. A single **PRINT** is preferred, however, because it saves memory.

What do you think changing the comma in line 10 to a semicolon will do? Try it, and you'll see 330, because the numbers are printed next to each other. This result is the same as that produced with **PRINT** 3;30 and is another example of concatenation. Note that **PRINT** 330 prints the number 330, but **PRINT** 3;30 prints two concatenated numbers.

The semicolon at the end of line 10 links this output to the next **PRINT** statement in the program. Notice that the next **PRINT** does not have to follow immediately the **PRINT** with the semicolon. For example,

    10 **PRINT** 5;
    20 **LET** X=10
    30 **PRINT** X

will print 510 since the intervening statement on line 20 does not affect the command on line 30. Of course, if X has not been defined, then you'll see an error message when the computer tries to execute line 30.

Saving Programs

Your computer's ability to save programs on tape can prevent a lot of program retyping. In addition, the values of variables can also be saved. Whatever you save is an exact copy of what was in your computer when the program was saved.

Let's try an example. First, enter the following program to compute the hypotenuse of a right triangle of sides 10 and 20:

    10 **LET** A=10
    20 **LET** B=20
    30 **LET** C=**SQR**(A**2+B**2)
    40 **PRINT** "HYPOTENUSE=";C

Run it, and you will see that the answer

    HYPOTENUSE=22.36068

appears at the top of your screen.

Now let's save this program on tape.

    (1) Connect the MIC jack on the recorder to the MIC jack on the computer. Remember that it is best to connect only one lead at a time, so don't connect a lead to the EAR jack.

    (2) Put a blank cassette tape in your recorder, or position a tape to the spot that you want to record over. It is

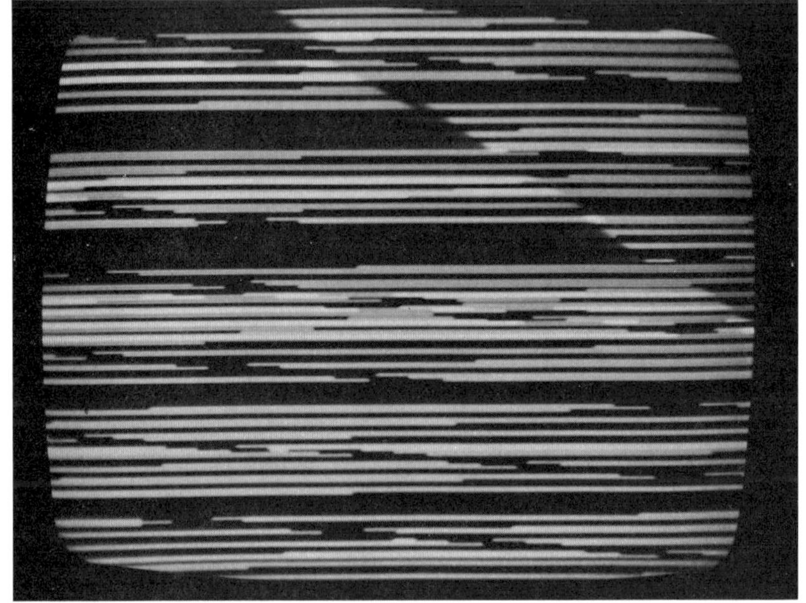

Figure 7-2
Saving a program.

advisable to buy high quality tapes for computer programs, since any imperfections may prevent your program from being reloaded. Check your local electronics store for computer-grade tapes.

(3) Press the **S** key. (The keyword **SAVE** should appear.)

(4) Give a name to the program. You can use any name of any length. For example, type in

SAVE "HYPO"

The name must be between quotation marks.

(5) Note the setting of the index counter of your tape recorder. Put the recorder on RECORD for a few seconds to allow the tape speed to stabilize. You don't want to start recording while the tape speed is changing, since this can lead to errors.

(6) After the recorder has been recording for a few seconds, press **ENTER**. The screen will go blank for about 5 seconds with some thin white lines dancing around the bottom of the screen. This pattern is followed by horizontal black and white stripes jumping around, indicating that output is going to the tape recorder (see Figure 7-2).

When the recording is over, the screen will go blank, and you will see a 0/0 in the bottom left corner. The program will still be in the computer's memory, which you can verify by doing a **LIST** command. Press the **K** key for **LIST**. Then press **ENTER** to see the program. The values of variables are still stored in the computer. Enter **PRINT** C, and you'll see 22.36068 printed.

You should verify that the program was recorded by listening to the tape. If a lead was not connected, or if you have a bad tape, then you won't get a recording. The pattern on the screen indicates only that information is being sent to the recorder. It does not indicate that the information was recorded. As you heard in Chapter 2, computer sounds are quite different from other sounds. Is the loudness of the sounds normal? Is there any unusual noise? If the tape sounds normal, and there's not a lot of background noise, you probably made a good copy. However, you should always have both a written copy and a duplicate tape as backups.

Now for the big test. Briefly pull the power plug out of the jack and then insert it again. Now load the program. You can load by entering

LOAD "HYPO"

anywhere before the program location on the tape. The computer will search through your tape for the first program called HYPO, then load it. You can also load by entering

LOAD ''''

Each quotation mark is made on the **P** key. The **LOAD** '''' command loads the next program, regardless of its name. Sometimes you'll have easier loading with the name, even if the tape is positioned close to the program.

You should always make two copies of a program, in case one doesn't turn out or gets accidentally erased. You can make the second copy on the same tape, but it is better to use a different one. The second copy is your backup, to be used only if something happens to the first copy. Should your first copy fail or get lost, load your backup tape into the computer and make a duplicate to be used as your replacement working copy.

There's nothing so frustrating as losing the only copy of your program after spending hours or days working on it. Sometimes such a loss can happen accidentally. For example, if the power plug is pulled out of the 9V D.C. jack, the computer will lose its memory. At other times, a program may get the computer into a condition in which it does not respond to commands. The only solution here is to pull the plug on purpose and start over. A third possibility is that, if the voltage in the power line fluctuates excessively because of heavy demand or noise on the line, the computer's memory contents will be erased. To reduce the size of a disaster like this, you should take the following precautions:

(1) Document every change to your program immediately after making it. Don't wait to try it out first.

(2) Make working copies on different portions of your tape. For example, when you enter a program into the computer from your written design, make a new copy after every 20 or 30 lines. Use a different portion of the tape for each copy, in case an accident happens during the copying.

(3) Use stick-on labels for your cassette to record the index counter's start and end settings, as well as the program's name. If you have several programs on a single tape, you may also want to tape a verbal description of each program to help you find it.

For good quality recordings, use shorter tapes, since there is less stretch in them and, therefore, less chance for error. Tapes such as C-10, C-15, or C-30 are usually long enough for many programs. In fact, using one tape for each program is ideal, since you won't have to waste time searching for a specific program. If you do a lot of programming, cassette storage boxes will help keep your tapes organized.

CHAPTER 8
Utility Commands

Certain commands called *utility commands* are helpful in organizing your work with the computer. They are especially useful in starting and stopping your program.

Running Your Program

By entering **RUN**, you get a program running, beginning with the lowest line number. However, you can start the running at any line by indicating the line number after **RUN**. Enter

        10 **PRINT** "LINE 10"
        20 **LET** X=1
        30 **PRINT** "X=";X
        40 **PRINT** "LINE 40"

and press **RUN**. You will see

        LINE 10
        X=1
        LINE 40

Now enter

    RUN 20

"LINE 10" will not be printed because you started running at line 20 instead of line 10. Now try

    RUN 30

This time all you will see is

    X=

and the error message 2/30. If you look up the report code of 2 in Appendix B, you will see that the problem is due to the use of a variable whose value has not been set by a **LET** statement. Since the computer started executing at line 30, it never executed line 20, in which the value of X was assigned.

Clearing Memory

By using the keyword **CLEAR**, located above the **X** key, you can erase the value assigned to a variable during execution. For example, enter and run the following new program:

    10 **LET** A=10

    20 **PRINT** A

You will see the value 10 appear. After any program is run, the variables retain the values they had when the program stopped.

Now enter

    CLEAR

and then

    PRINT A

A report code of 2 will appear, because the computer thinks you're trying to use a variable that has no value assigned. If you **LIST** the program, you will see that it is still in memory. The

CLEAR command makes the computer forget the value it had assigned to each variable.

Computer Memory Areas

The memory of your computer is divided into three main areas:

(1) The *program memory*—where the characters of your program are stored. BASIC uses special codes for commands so that a whole command, such as **PRINT**, is stored as a single number called a *token*. Using a token reduces the amount of memory a program requires, and makes it easier for the computer to execute a program. When the computer sees the token for **PRINT**, it knows immediately that you mean the command **PRINT**. Execution would be much slower if the computer had to check all the time for commands stored letter by letter.

(2) The *display file*—the TV screen can show a maximum of 22 lines of 32 characters each for your program and output. This requires 22*32 = 704 bytes of storage. The 23rd line is blank to separate the top 22 lines from the bottom line. The bottom 24th line is used for editing and inputting lines, not for displaying program output. Twenty-four **ENTER** characters are used to mark the end of lines, and one is used to mark the beginning of the first line. If you have less than 3 1/4 K of memory, the display file is compressed to the minimum size required to show what is on the screen. Generally, with the 16K RAM Module, the display is kept expanded to its maximum size. The absolute minimum is 25 characters after a **CLS** command, plus the report code/line number 0/0 on the bottom line of your screen. The more you display, the more memory you need. To conserve memory, print on the top left side of the screen. Tabs and spaces require additional memory for the display file.

(3) The *variable area*—where the value assigned to each variable is stored during program execution. A numeric variable requires 5 bytes for the numeric value and one byte for each character of the variable

name. A string variable requires 3 bytes for the name, plus 1 byte for each character in the string. In addition, 125 bytes are needed by BASIC itself. Also, other memory may be required during program execution for temporary storage. For example, the use of parentheses forces the computer to store results temporarily.

The minimum memory needed to run a nontrivial program is about 1K bytes. Obviously, the more available memory a computer has, the better off you will be in programming. If only a small amount of memory is available, you may spend most of your time trying to squeeze your program into it. Some people enjoy doing this as a challenge.

A way to use memory efficiently is to employ variables in place of constants. A *constant* is a number or string whose value does not change. For example, at several places in a program you may have

        20 **LET** A=10*B

        . . . .

        . . . .
        50 **LET** Q=10+X
        60 **LET** A=A+Q/10

        . . . .
        80 **PRINT** 10+TOTAL

Notice that the number 10 appears in each illustrated line. In the program area, a number such as 10 uses 1 byte for each character, 5 bytes for its value, and 1 byte for a code to show that 10 is a number. Therefore, it takes 8 bytes of storage each time a 10 is used in the program. Since 10 appears 4 times in the illustration above, 10 as a constant uses 32 bytes (4*8 = 32). To economize, you could define a variable as follows:

        5 **LET** T=10

The entire statement requires 16 bytes in program area storage, as shown in the following table:

Program Area Storage

Item Description	Item	Bytes
Line number	5	2
Length of line		2
Command	**LET**	1
Variable name	T	1
Operator	=	1
Value	10	2+6
ENTER		1
TOTAL		16

Six bytes are required by line 5 in variable area storage, as follows:

Variable Area Storage

Item Description	Item	Bytes
Variable name	T	1
Value	10	5
TOTAL		6

If we add line 5 to the program, we add 22 bytes (16+6 = 22); but now, we will use only one byte each time we use T instead of 10.

For example,

```
 5 LET T=10
20 LET A=T*B
. . . . . . . . .
. . . . . . . . .
50 LET Q=T+X
60 LET A=A+Q/T
. . . . . . . . .
. . . . . . . . .
```

        80 **PRINT** T+TOTAL

Here, 7 bytes of memory are saved each time T replaces 10 in lines 20, 50, 60, and 80. That means a saving of 28 bytes (4*7 = 28).

Since it took 22 bytes to enter the variable in line 5, the net amount of memory saved so far is 6 bytes (28-22 = 6). The net amount saved will increase significantly if T and other such variables are used frequently in a long program. As a general rule, *if a constant is used often, substituting a variable can conserve memory.*

Also, the constant **PI** can be used to save memory. For example, if you need the constant 1 as in

        LET T=1

then you can use

        LET T=**PI/PI**

since any number divided by itself equals 1.

Only 3 bytes are needed to store **PI/PI** as opposed to the 6 or more bytes required to store a number, because a one-byte token is used for each **PI** as well as for the / sign.

If you need a 0 in your program, you can use

        LET T=**PI-PI**

which will save 5 bytes of memory.

Clearing Things Up

If your memory area is very limited, you can include **CLEAR** as a program statement. This statement will release the variable storage space used by previous variables. For example, enter

        10 **LET** A=10
        20 **PRINT** A
        30 **CLEAR**

        40 **LET** B=5
        50 **PRINT** B

as your program and run it. It will execute normally and print out A and B. However, less space is used in the variable area during execution with the addition of line 30. Be careful not to refer to variable A after the **CLEAR** if line 30 was executed, because the computer will give you a report code error of 2. For example, enter

        60 **PRINT** A

and run. Only a 10 and a 5 will be printed. The computer will stop with the report code/line number 2/60 when it encounters the last **PRINT** A, because the **CLEAR** command has cleared the computer's memory of A's value.

When you consider using **CLEAR** in a program, you should also consider its storage. A line number needs 2 bytes of storage, while **CLEAR** and **ENTER** need 1 byte each. An additional 2 bytes are used in storing the length of the line. Thus, by adding

        30 **CLEAR**

you have increased the program memory required by 6 bytes and reduced the variable memory required by only 5 bytes. Therefore, if you have only 1 variable, it is not worth adding a **CLEAR** to your program.

A **CLEAR** can be useful in another area. If you finish running a program and want to save it on cassette, a **CLEAR** will decrease the amount of data to be stored. When you store a program that's just been run, the last values of all the variables are also stored. In some cases, you may want to store these values. For example, you may run a checkbook balancing program in which you want to save the values of check amounts, check numbers, dates, and payees. In other cases, you may want only to save the program itself. Saving the program alone uses less space on the cassette and takes less time to save and read back from tape.

A New Start

List the program on your TV screen. Now press the keyword **NEW**, located above the **A** key, and then **ENTER**. This command deletes a program from memory. It also clears the display file and the variable storage area. The **NEW** command resets the computer to the place where you started originally—with nothing in memory. It is better to use **NEW** when you want to start over than to pull the plug on your computer. The **NEW** command does not put the wear and tear on the computer hardware that pulling the plug does.

A Running Stop

To stop a program that is running, insert a **STOP** statement. The **STOP** is made by shifting the **A** key. Enter and run

        10 **LET** A=10
        20 **PRINT** A
        30 **LET** B=5
        40 **PRINT** B

Then enter and run

        35 **STOP**

The program will stop at line 35 with a report code of 9/35. If you look up report code 9 in Appendix C, you will see that 9 means a **STOP** was encountered.

The **RUN** (followed by an optional line number) and **STOP** commands can also be used when you are storing several different programs in memory at the same time. If you have enough memory, you can store an educational program with lines 10 to 100, a game program with lines 120 to 250, and a business program with lines 270 to 500. You can then run any of these programs by entering **RUN** and the line number. Using **RUN** saves you the trouble of entering each program separately into memory when you want to use it. Entering **STOP** after each program will keep you from accidentally running into the next one.

Going Somewhere

The **GOTO** command, located as a keyword above the **G** key, can be used as a utility command as well as in statements. As its name implies, the **GOTO** command makes the computer *go to* a line and start executing from that line. However, there is one big difference between **RUN** and **GOTO**: **GOTO** does not clear the value assigned to a variable. For example, if you run the program below, the value 5 will be printed.

        10 **LET** A=5

        20 **PRINT** A

Now enter a **LET** command

        LET A=10   (and press **ENTER**)

then enter

        GOTO 20

and you will see a value of 10 printed for A. If you had tried

        RUN 20

an error code would have appeared, because **RUN** clears the variable memory area.

Include and run the following statement

        30 **GOTO** 20

and you will see a column of fives march down the screen. The computer executes lines 10 to 30, then goes back to line 20 and prints A, again and again, until one of two things happens:

(1) The display fills up with the report code/line number 5/20, meaning the screen is full, so execution stopped at line 20. If you want to continue, just press the **CONT** key (and **ENTER**). **CONT** is a keyword over the **C** key. The screen will be cleared, and you will start executing again at the line after 20.

(2) You press the **BREAK** key. **BREAK** is a command located over the **SPACE** key. You can't print the **BREAK** command. It is used only for interrupting a program—it breaks the execution. Run the program, then press **BREAK**. The output will stop.

Of course, you can always pull the plug to stop execution. But if you do, the program is lost from memory. However, if **BREAK** does not stop execution, pulling the plug is the only solution.

The End of the Universe

One theory of cosmic evolution predicts that some stars will blow up and collapse into black holes from which nothing can escape, not even light. As time passes, more black holes will form that will ultimately devour the universe. Let's simulate the growth of black holes with the following program:

```
10 LET X=INT(21*RND+.5)
20 LET Y=INT(31*RND+.5)
30 PRINT AT X,Y;"*"
40 GOTO 10
```

Lines 10 and 20 illustrate how you can generate a random whole number between limits. In line 10, a random number X is generated, where $0<=X<=21$. This notation means that X can take a value greater than or equal to 0, and less than or equal to 21. Recall that the **RND** function generates a number greater than or equal to 0, and less than 1. This is expressed by

$$0<=\textbf{RND}<1$$

Multiplying through by 21 will give you a number greater than or equal to 0, and less than 21. This is shown by

$$0<=21*\textbf{RND}<21$$

Adding .5 gives

$$0.5<=21*\textbf{RND}+.5<21.5$$

Taking the integer part gives

$$0 < \ = INT \ (21*RND + .5) < \ = 21$$

which shows that we are generating a random whole number from 0 through 21.

In line 20, a random number Y is generated, where $0 < \ = Y < \ = 31$. The factors of 21 and 31 in lines 10 and 20 were chosen so that the **PRINT AT** coordinates X and Y in line 30 would be within their valid ranges: $0 = \ < X < \ = 21$, $0 = \ < Y < \ = 31$. Otherwise, one of our black holes would exceed the boundaries of our "universe," the valid range for the **PRINT AT** command.

Run this program, and you will see asterisks appear on the screen as the black holes devour the universe. If you only have 1K bytes of memory in your computer, as with the Sinclair ZX-81, eventually you will see a report code of 4, meaning the computer is out of memory. If you do, just cut down the size of the universe by changing the factor 31 to 30 in line 20. The display file has expanded so much that there is not enough memory left in the computer to continue executing. With the standard 2K bytes of memory in the T/S 1000, you won't have this problem.

Speeding Up the End

Your T/S 1000 can operate about four times faster by being put in the **FAST** mode. The **FAST** command is a shifted **F**. Enter **FAST**, then run the preceding program. Notice that the screen goes blank while the program is running. This happens because your computer is spending all of its time on calculations instead of on refreshing the TV screen.

The term *refreshing* refers to the rewriting of the picture on the screen, which must be done at 60 frames a second. Otherwise, you would see no picture. In your computer a device called a Z80 microprocessor controls all of the computer's activities. In standard **SLOW** mode, the microprocessor must continually interrupt its calculations to refresh the screen. In **FAST** mode, the microprocessor concentrates on the calculations alone. To return to **SLOW** mode, press the shifted **D** key. **SLOW** and **FAST** can also be included as statements in your program. When you need the speed and don't care about the display, use **FAST**. When you need to see the display, switch to **SLOW**.

The PAUSE That Refreshes

The **PAUSE** command, located as a keyword over the **M** key, stops calculations and shows the display. **PAUSE** halts execution in units of one TV frame. Two frames make up a complete picture on your screen. The image for a standard U.S. TV transmission is formed at the rate of 60 frames per second; therefore, the smallest unit for a **PAUSE** is 1/60 of a second. The maximum number of pauses allowed is 65,535. Pauses from 32,767 to 65,535 are not timed. Instead, you press a key to terminate the **PAUSE**. In fact, you can always terminate a **PAUSE** by pressing any key.

Let's try timing a **PAUSE**. Since one frame = 1/60 second, 20 seconds should equal 1,200 frames. Enter

>   **PAUSE** 1200

Note that everything disappears from the screen. Time your **PAUSE** from when you press the **ENTER** key until a 0/0 appears.

The problem with using a **PAUSE** in your program is that other statements will affect the time. For example, enter

>   10 **LET** N=0
>   20 **PAUSE** 60
>   30 **PRINT AT** 0,0;N
>   40 **LET** N=N+1
>   50 **GOTO** 20

This program acts as a digital timer. About every second, it prints the elapsed time in seconds since the program started. Although a **PAUSE** lasts one second, the computer does take some time to execute the other statements. To compensate for the difference, you have to adjust the **PAUSE** 60 downward. Unfortunately, the smallest increment you can adjust is 1/60 seconds, and this may not be accurate over a long period. Another problem with **PAUSE** is the annoying screen flicker that occurs when it reactivates the screen.

Debugging

A program with errors is said to have *bugs* in it. *Debugging* is the process of finding and correcting these errors.

If you think a program works correctly up to a certain point, you can put a **STOP** after the good code, then print out the values of the variables. By checking the values stored in the computer against what they should be, you can isolate the bug to a small portion of the program code. Sometimes you may need to put several **STOP**'s in the program if you're not sure exactly where the problem is. Simply press **CONT** to continue program execution after each **STOP**. You may also want to add temporary **PRINT** statements to your program to print out automatically the values of the variables as the program continues to execute.

And Now, a Brief Remark

When you write a program, it is helpful to include comments about what the program is doing. These comments are particularly useful when you use short variable names or write tricky code to conserve space. After a few months, even the person who wrote the original code may have trouble understanding it.

You can add remarks to your program using the keyword **REM**, located just above the **E** key. Enter and run

```
10 REM PROGRAM TO ADD NUMBERS
20 PRINT 10+20
```

Notice that your only output is the answer 30. The **REM** statement can be listed with the program, but does not print any output. It is useful to document your programs with remark statements.

If you, or someone else, want to change a program, particularly one that you wrote some time ago and stored on tape, it is very difficult to do so with little or no documentation.

The advantage of a **REM** is that it is always stored with your program. Whereas documentation on paper may get lost, internal documentation does not, because it is part of the program. Two disadvantages of using REM statements are a need for additional memory for the **REM** line and a decrease in execution speed. The execution speed is decreased because the **REM** statement must first be recognized by the computer before the statement can be ignored. To the computer, **REM** is like a sign that says, "Ignore this sign."

When you use remark statements, try to make them meaningful and short, since each character uses one byte of memory. Don't just say

        10 **REM PRINT** SUM OF A AND B

        20 **PRINT** A + B

Instead, try to give an idea of what the next section of the program should do. If the 32 characters on one line aren't enough, continue the thought on the next line with another **REM**.

A **REM** is also useful for inserting a copyright claim into a program that you've written. For example, you could enter

        10 **REM** (C) COPYRIGHT 1983

        20 **REM** BY JOHN SMITH

        30 **REM** ALL RIGHTS RESERVED

at the beginning of a program as part of the formal copyright procedure. (Of course, you would also have to fill out the official government copyright forms.)

CHAPTER 9
Giving the Computer Input

Thus far, we have discussed giving the computer data with a **LET** statement. This method usually requires modifying the program, which is not very efficient if you're trying to run the same program all the time on different data.

Supplying Data without Changing the Program

One way to supply data without modifying your program is to enter a **LET** command while the program is stopped. For example,

    10 **STOP**

    20 **PRINT** A

Run this program, and you will see it stop at line 10. Now enter

    LET A = 5

    CONT

The result 5 will be printed on your screen. This example illustrates how easy it is to change and examine the values of variables when your program is not running. If you're short of memory space, you can even **LET** the values of variables in this manner without having to enter program lines.

Notice that we used a **STOP** and a **CONT** in the preceding example. A single line

  10 **PRINT** A

followed by

  LET A=5
  RUN

would not have worked because the **RUN** clears the values assigned to all variables before the computer starts executing lines. But **GOTO** 10 would have worked instead of **RUN**.

The INPUT Command

The **INPUT** command, the keyword over the I key, serves the same purpose as the **STOP** and **LET** commands. Try this example:

  10 **INPUT** A
  20 **PRINT** A

and run it. At first, you may think nothing has happened. But notice that an **L** prompt has appeared in the bottom left corner of your screen. The **L** means that the computer has understood the **INPUT** statement and is waiting for you to give it a number. Type in a 10 and press the **ENTER** key. You will see a 10 appear in the upper left corner of the screen and the report code/line number 0/20, meaning the program successfully stopped executing with line 20.

To use your program, an illustration of what is expected for input is helpful. For example, enter and run

  10 **PRINT** "DIVIDEND=?";
  20 **INPUT** X

```
30 PRINT X
40 PRINT "DIVISOR=?";
50 INPUT Y
60 PRINT Y
70 PRINT "QUOTIENT=";X/Y
```

Using the numbers 10 for dividend and 5 for divisor, you will see

```
DIVIDEND=?10
DIVISOR=?5
QUOTIENT=2
```

Notice how the semicolons at the end of lines 10 and 40, and in line 70, were used to force the printing of the next output on the same line. Try the same program without the semicolons, and you'll see on the screen the inputs printed on the next line.

Now try entering a character, such as A, instead of a number. As you can see, the result is an error message. You can input a string, but it must be assigned to a string variable. For example, try

```
10 PRINT "FIRST NAME=?";
20 INPUT F$
30 PRINT F$
40 PRINT "SECOND NAME=?";
50 INPUT S$
60 PRINT S$
70 PRINT "FULL NAME=";F$+S$
```

Run this example, using your name as the input. Notice that there are now quotation marks around the **L** prompt, showing that the computer expects a string.

Although the program works, the output looks funny because there is no space between your first and second names. To correct this problem, enter the line

```
70 PRINT "FULL NAME=";F$+"   "+S$
```

Now a blank space will be inserted between your first and second names. How would you modify line 70 to print your last name, a comma, and then your first name?

The **INPUT** command is more powerful than it appears at first.

Enter the program

    10 **INPUT** A

    20 **PRINT** A

    30 **GOTO** 10

and run it, using the following expressions:

Example	Answer
7-5	2
3*4-6	6
2**3+1.4/1.3	9.079231
8.09***SIN** (2***PI**/3)	7.0061455

A feature of T/S 1000 BASIC is its ability to reduce any expression you input to a number.

An Input Loop

By combining the **INPUT** and **GOTO** commands, you can write a program that looks continuously for input. Enter and run the following program for different numbers:

    10 **INPUT** A

    20 **PRINT** A

    30 **GOTO** 10

Once a number is entered, the program will always execute lines 10, 20, and 30, then return to line 10.

If its hardware never broke down, and you kept giving input, the computer would stay within lines 10, 20, and 30 forever. It would be *caught in a loop.*

But how do you stop such a program, other than by pulling the plug and erasing the program from memory? If the **GOTO** command goes to a non-**INPUT** statement, you can stop the program by pressing the **BREAK** key. Or if the **GOTO** goes to line 20, the computer will automatically stop execution when the screen becomes full. However, if you try pressing **BREAK** when the computer is expecting input, you will only input a space.

You can stop the **INPUT** request by entering a **STOP** in response to the request. This BASIC is so designed that a **STOP** will terminate execution with a report code of D. Another way to stop this program is to enter a non-number, such as X. The computer can't assign a character to a numeric variable, so the computer will stop with a report code of 2.

What happens if your program inputs a string? Try

> 10 **INPUT** A$
>
> 20 **PRINT** A$
>
> 30 **GOTO** 10

using inputs of A, JOE, 23.8, -9, and **STOP.** You will see that everything you input is accepted, even **STOP.** If the screen fills up, the program will stop and give a report code of 5. If you want to stop the program without having to fill the screen, you have to

(1) delete the quotation mark to the left of the **L** by pressing **SHIFT** and **DELETE**

(2) press the keyword **STOP**, then press **ENTER**. Now the program will stop with a report code of D. You have stopped the program by entering **STOP** at the beginning of the **INPUT** line. Deleting the first quotation mark in the line was necessary so that **STOP** could be entered.

Reading the Keyboard

The **INPUT** command is useful for calculations or other data processing in which you want the computer to stop, wait for input, then continue execution. However, in designing games, you may want the computer to respond without stopping the program to ask for input. A familiar example is the joystick of a video game. The game machine continues to respond as you move the joystick, instead of halting the action to ask for input.

Your computer has under the **B** key a shifted string function called **INKEY$**, which can be used to tell automatically what key is pressed. If a key is pressed, the **INKEY$** function returns either its character or the *null string*. The null string is ''"'', meaning no character. Now enter and run the following program, pressing different keys to see what happens:

```
10 LET K$ = INKEY$
20 PRINT K$;
30 GOTO 10
```

An even shorter version is

```
10 PRINT INKEY$
20 GOTO 10
```

and a shorter version still is

```
10 PRINT INKEY$
20 RUN
```

Notice how quickly **INKEY$** scans the keyboard. Can you press a key just long enough to print one character? Question marks appear for keys that are not printable symbols, such as **ENTER** and **EDIT**.

Scrolling Along

When you write a program to input data, the program will stop when the screen is full. For example, enter this program to calculate square roots:

```
10 INPUT A
20 PRINT SQR A
30 GOTO 10
```

Keep entering numbers until the screen is full and you get the report code/line number 5/20. If you want to continue inputting, you must press **CONT**.

Your computer has a command that can prevent a full screen from occurring. Add

15 **SCROLL**

to your program. **SCROLL** is a keyword above the **B** key. Now when you run this program, the output will appear on the bottom line of the screen and scroll upward.

SCROLL moves the top line off the screen and sets the printing position to the bottom line, 21. If you enter **SCROLL** as a command, it will only clear the screen.

CHAPTER 10
Tests and Decisions

A major advantage of a computer over a simple calculator is the computer's ability to make tests and decisions. The computer can respond to changes in the data and take the appropriate action.

The IF Command

The BASIC **IF** command, used with the keyword **THEN**, can perform tests and decisions. **IF** is a keyword over the **U** key, and **THEN** is a shifted **3** key. Try

        10 **INPUT** A$

        20 **IF** A$ = "DONE" **THEN STOP**

        30 **PRINT** A$

        40 **GOTO** 10

As each string is entered, it will be printed on the screen. To stop your program, simply type in the word DONE. Using an **IF** command in this manner allows a more orderly exit from a program than deleting the left quotation mark and entering **STOP.**

The general format of an **IF** statement is **IF** (test) **THEN** (statement). The **IF** checks to see if the test or condition is true. If it is true, then the statement is executed. If the test is not true, then the line following this **IF** statement is executed. The "test" often involves one of the relational operators:

Symbol	Meaning	Shifted Key
=	Equal	**L**
<=	Less than or equal to	**R**
<>	Unequal	**T**
>=	Greater than or equal to	**Y**
<	Less than	**N**
>	Greater than	**M**

To use one of these relational operators, press the appropriate shifted key, as shown in the table above. Remember that if you try to combine these operators, you will get a syntax error message. For example, if you first press the shifted **N** and then the shifted **M** keys, a $<>$ will appear on the screen, but will not be accepted. You must use the shifted **T** key for $<>$.

The use of relational operators is shown in the following examples:

> **IF** 1$<$2 **THEN LET** A$=$A$+$3
>
> **IF** (X*3-3)$<>$R***SIN** Z **THEN GOTO** 500
>
> **IF** A\$$=$"BOB"$+$"TED" **THEN PRINT** "YES"
>
> **IF** Q\$$<>$C\$ **THEN STOP**

Notice that we always test a relationship and follow it with a statement. Numeric variables are always compared to numeric variables, and strings are always compared to strings. In other words, you can't mix apples and oranges.

Going Out in Style

The **IF** test allows you to go out of a program in style. Instead of inputting **STOP**, you can have the program look for a specific input and then stop. For example, try

```
10 PRINT "MORE INPUT? YES OR NO"
20 INPUT A$
30 IF A$="YES" THEN GOTO 50
40 STOP
50 PRINT A$
60 GOTO 10
```

Lines 50 through 60 can be replaced by whatever calculations you want to make. In the program above, line 50 prints YES only if you answer yes. Otherwise, the program will stop with report code/line number 9/40.

You may want to change the 60 **GOTO** 10 to 9999 **GOTO** 10. Now you are using the highest line number available to the T/S 1000 BASIC. All other program lines for calculations must be less than 9999. Using line 9999 makes the last statement in your program loop back to the first. You can insert other lines for the program after line 50. Those lines are executed only if A$="YES."

Another way to end your program is to print a message. For example, add

```
35 PRINT "PROGRAM END"
```

If you just want to stop without a message, you can replace line 30 by

```
30 IF A$="NO" THEN STOP
```

and delete line 40 **STOP**. The single line **IF . . . STOP** saves memory space, compared to the two-line version.

Your Mean Machine

Let's look at a program to calculate the *mean*, or *average*, of numbers. Determining the mean is done by adding up numbers and dividing the total by how many numbers you used. For example, if you use the numbers 1, 2, and 3, the mean is

$$(1+2+3)/3=2$$

The general formula for finding the mean of numbers is

$$\text{MEAN} = \frac{N1 + N2 + N3 + ...Nmax}{MAX} = \frac{SUM}{MAX}$$

in which the numbers are N1, N2, N3, on up to the maximum number Nmax. For our example above,

> N1 = 1
>
> N2 = 2
>
> N3 = 3 = Nmax
>
> SUM = 6
>
> MAX = 3
>
> SUM/MAX = 2 = AVERAGE

The three dots after the " + " in the formula above indicate that as many terms as are necessary up to Nmax are included.

Following is one program you can use to find the mean with your machine:

```
 5 REM COMPUTE MEAN
10 PRINT "HOW MANY NUMBERS?";
20 INPUT MAX
30 PRINT MAX
40 LET COUNT=0
50 LET SUM=0
60 SCROLL
70 LET COUNT=COUNT+1
80 PRINT COUNT;"-NUMBER=";
90 INPUT N
100 PRINT N
110 LET SUM=SUM+N
120 IF COUNT<MAX THEN GOTO 60
130 SCROLL
140 PRINT "MEAN=";SUM/MAX
```

Line 10 asks how many numbers there will be (= MAX).

You could write another version of this program that would process numbers until a special one is read, say, 1E38. Pick a value that's unlikely to be present and keep track of how many numbers are input. When your special number appears, it will act as a flag in an **IF** test that will set the number of values read in up to that point as MAX.

In our Mean program, the variable COUNT keeps track of how many numbers are input. Line 120 checks to see if COUNT is less than MAX. If it is, the program will loop back to line 60 and get ready to input another number. In lines 60 and 130, we **SCROLL** the input numbers, because if only **PRINT** were used, you would have to press **CONT** each time the screen filled up with input. (It's annoying to have to use the **CONT** command repeatedly if you have many values to input.)

Line 80 acts as a check on the input. It prints how many numbers should have been input. For example, if your data were 8, 3, and 16.7, you'd see

```
1-NUMBER = 8
2-NUMBER = 3
3-NUMBER = 16.7
. . . . . . .
. . . . . . .
```

If the maximum number of items doesn't equal the value of COUNT that's printed, then you've probably skipped a number. Line 110 calculates the sum of all the numbers that have been input. This is the way a sum of numbers in a loop is usually calculated. Line 140 prints the mean.

Months and Days

The **IF** command can be used in a program that will give you the number of days in a month when you input its number.

```
5 REM MONTH NUMBERS
```

```
 10 PRINT "NUMBER OF MONTH=?";
 20 INPUT N
 30 PRINT N
 40 IF N=1 THEN PRINT 31
 50 IF N=2 THEN PRINT 28
 60 IF N=3 THEN PRINT 31
 70 IF N=4 THEN PRINT 30
 80 IF N=5 THEN PRINT 31
 90 IF N=6 THEN PRINT 30
100 IF N=7 THEN PRINT 31
110 IF N=8 THEN PRINT 31
120 IF N=9 THEN PRINT 30
130 IF N=10 THEN PRINT 31
140 IF N=11 THEN PRINT 30
150 IF N=12 THEN PRINT 31
160 IF N>12 THEN STOP
170 IF N<1 THEN STOP
180 GOTO 10
```

Notice that you can stop the program in line 160 or line 170 by entering an N that is greater than 12 or less than 1. These lines also serve as a means of checking input errors, since the months can only be numbered 1 through 12 here. It is better to plan for a possible error than to have your program suddenly crash. The term *crash* is a computer expression for an unplanned breakdown of the computer hardware or software. Crashes are not popular because they may cause the loss of a program or data. To avoid such losses, it is always a good idea to have a copy of your program stored.

The program above will simply stop when it recognizes an error. To prevent the program from crashing to a stop if you enter an error, you can amend the program by entering the following:

```
160 IF N>12 THEN GOTO 500
```

```
170 IF N<12 THEN GOTO 520

500 PRINT "MONTH GREATER THAN 12. PLEASE RE-
    ENTER"

510 GOTO 10

520 PRINT "MONTH LESS THAN 1. PLEASE RE-ENTER"

530 GOTO 10
```

It is very annoying to get an error message or a cryptic message when an error occurs. Now, with the changes in lines 160 and 170, you will get clear explanations of error messages. It is not enough to design a program that works with perfect input. You also have to figure a method of *program recovery,* or a way to keep a program going when input is not correct.

What would the output be if lines 160 and 170 were not present and you input a 13? Try it and see.

We can also modify this program to adjust for a leap year. Enter these lines:

```
50 IF N=2 THEN GOTO 190

190 PRINT "LEAP YEAR? YES OR NO";

200 INPUT A$

210 IF A$="NO" THEN GOTO 240

220 PRINT 29

230 GOTO 10

240 PRINT 28

250 GOTO 10
```

Line 50 sends the computer to line 190 if the input is 2. Line 190 asks if you want the number of days in February for a leap year. Your answer is stored in the string variable A$. If it is not a leap year, line 210 sends the computer to line 240, **PRINT** 28. If the A$ is "YES," then the computer will execute line 220 instead of going to line 240, and a 29 will be printed for the number of days in February for a leap year.

Instead of asking for the number of the month as input in your program, you can use the names of the months. Try the following:

```
5 REM MONTHS AND DAYS
10 PRINT "ENTER MONTH";
20 INPUT M$
30 PRINT M$
40 IF M$="JANUARY" THEN PRINT 31
50 IF M$="FEBRUARY" THEN PRINT 28
60 IF M$="MARCH" THEN PRINT 31
70 IF M$="APRIL" THEN PRINT 30
80 IF M$="MAY" THEN PRINT 31
90 IF M$="JUNE" THEN PRINT 30
100 IF M$="JULY" THEN PRINT 31
110 IF M$="AUGUST" THEN PRINT 31
120 IF M$="SEPTEMBER" THEN PRINT 30
130 IF M$$="OCTOBER" THEN PRINT 31
140 IF M$$="NOVEMBER" THEN PRINT 30
150 IF M$$="DECEMBER" THEN PRINT 31
160 GOTO 10
```

Notice that in this version, there is no error checking. If you input a word that does not satisfy any **IF** test in lines 40 through 150, then nothing is printed, just as when lines 160 and 170 were removed from the preceding program.

A program using the names of the months is pretty slow, because even if it finds the right month, it must still try all the others. You can speed up the program at the expense of more memory by using **GOTO**'s. Try to modify your program in this way. Be sure you include a version of the test for leap years in your program.

Fixing Cracks and Building Skyscrapers

Unless you're writing a program of only a few lines, it is best to write up a plan of how the program will work. There are two ways to plan; they can be used separately or together.

The first method is to write a general algorithm. For example, to compute the days of the month,

1. Input the number of the month
2. If it matches a month, then print the number of days
3. Else print an error message
4. Start over

A description like this is called *pseudocode,* which literally means *false code.* You can't enter it directly into the computer as BASIC code, yet it has a direct relationship to the BASIC code you will

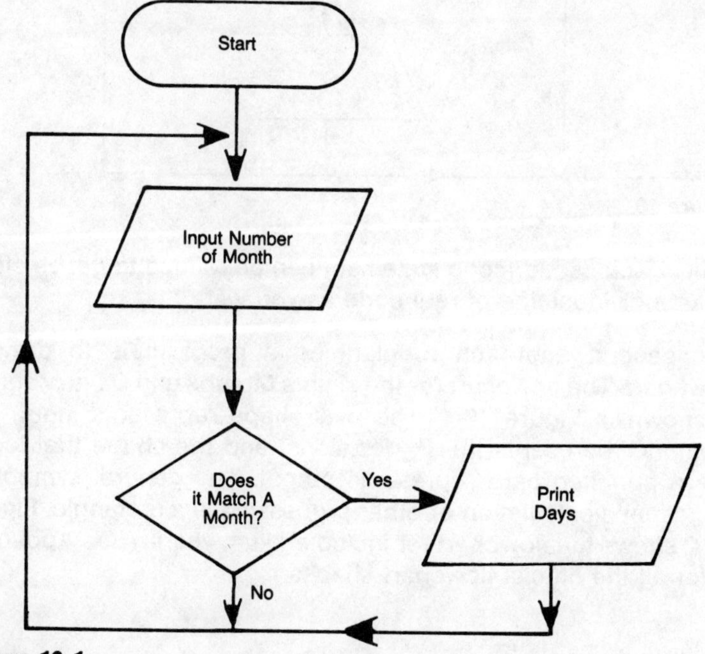

Figure 10-1

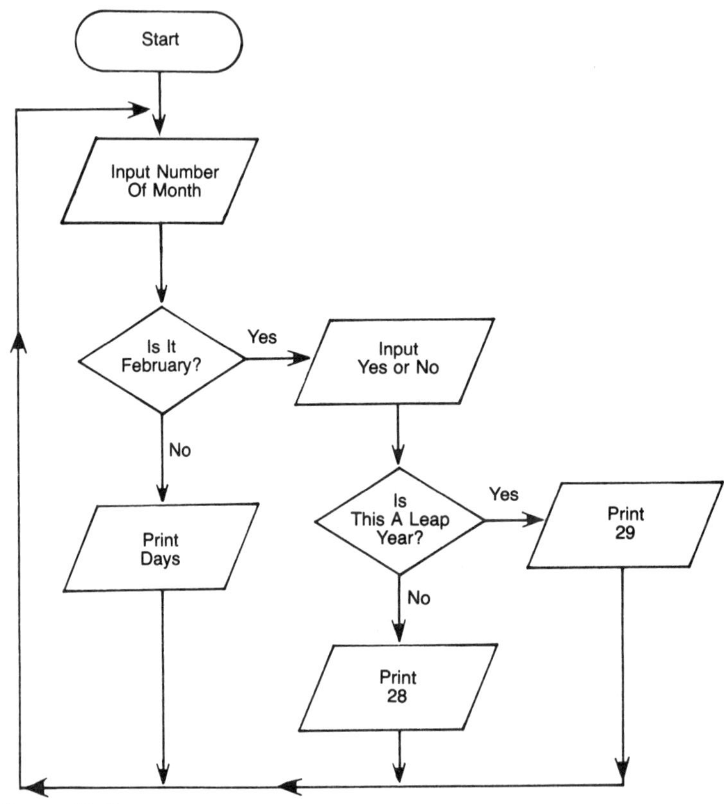

Figure 10-2

write. Each pseudocode statement can be refined to get as close to an individual line of real code as you want.

The second approach to planning a program is to draw a *flowchart*. The flowchart for the simple Months and Days program is shown in Figure 10-1. The oval shape represents input, the diamond represents the **IF** decisions, and the shape that looks like a punched card represents output. The general symbol to represent a calculation or other processing is a rectangle. Figure 10-2 shows the flowchart for including leap years. (See Appendix D for all the official flowchart shapes.)

Some companies require a flowchart for each program. However, the flowchart for a large program can be quite complex. Try both flowcharts and pseudocode when you write programs to see which you prefer. The important thing is that you plan the structure of a program before writing the code. Without a good foundation, you could spend most of your time fixing cracks rather than building skyscrapers.

Who's Touching My Keyboard?

Now let's use the **IF** to control **INKEY$**. Try this program:

```
10 IF INKEY$ ="" THEN GOTO 10
20 PRINT INKEY$
30 IF INKEY$ <>"" THEN GOTO 30
40 GOTO 10
```

Notice that the null string "" in lines 10 and 30 is typed by pressing the shifted **P** twice. You'll get a syntax error if you use the shifted **Q**, because that key is for the quote image and is used to print a quotation mark.

With this program, only one character is printed each time you press a key. Now you can determine a single touch on the keyboard.

Line 10 of the program checks to see if a key is being pressed. Since we're starting off this program by holding down the **ENTER** key, we move on to line 20. This line prints a ? at the top of the screen since there is no printable character defined in BASIC for **ENTER**. Then the program goes to line 30. If your finger is still on the **ENTER** key, the computer will just loop back to this same line until you let go. When you do let go, the program will go to line 40 and loop back to line 10, and so on. Can you think up another version of this program that will not print the first **ENTER**?

Drawing Pictures

You can easily draw pictures on the screen by using the commands we've discussed so far. Try this program to draw a vertical line of asterisks:

```
10 LET X=11
20 LET Y=16
30 LET K$=INKEY$
40 IF K$="6" THEN LET X=X+1
50 IF K$="7" THEN LET X=X-1
60 PRINT AT X,Y;"*"
70 GOTO 30
```

Of course, you can substitute any character for the asterisk. Try some graphics characters, too.

Lines 10 and 20 initialize the first character to about the center of the screen. Lines 40 and 50 check the value of **INKEY$** against the characters "6" and "7." These characters were picked because the **6** key has a down arrow printed on it, and the **7** key has an up arrow. These keys are often used in games for controlling up and down movement, while the **5** and **8** keys are used to control left and right. Line 60 prints an asterisk for the cursor at the X,Y position, and line 70 loops back for a new **INKEY$**.

If you start moving the cursor from the center of the screen to the top, the cursor will start moving back down after it reaches the screen boundary at X=0. When the cursor reaches the top, nothing happens for a few seconds because the cursor is retracing its path, and no change is visible. Eventually, you will see the cursor move down past the center of the screen as you keep pressing the **7** key. Finally, the program will stop with a report code of 5 as the cursor tries to go past the bottom of the screen.

You can see the values of X if you insert this line into the program:

```
65 PRINT AT 18,0;X
```

The initial value of X will be 11, which you will see in the bottom left corner of your screen. As you press the **7** key, this value will change to 11, 10, 90, 80, 70, 60, 50, 40, 30, 20, 10, 0, -10. . . . The printed value of X is displayed falsely when X changes from 10 to 9. The 9 appears to be 90 because the 9 is placed over the 1 of 10, and the 0 of 10 remains visible to the right of the 9. The reason why this misleading image appears is that the **PRINT AT** command in line 65 prints X in column 0—the location of the 1 of 10— at the far left of the screen. Because the 0 is still visible, the value of X seems to change in units of 10, (90, 80, 70, etc.) although it really does not. A better way would be to add an additional line:

      62 **PRINT AT** 18,0;" "

in which the blanks between quotation marks wipe out the previous number. Then when line 65 is printed, no false image appears. When the cursor's X value reaches 0, it has reached the upper limit of the screen. When 1 is subtracted from 0 to give -1, the cursor starts backtracking down the screen. The last value allowed is X = 21 before execution stops with a report code of 5.

If you add lines for horizontal movement, such as

      45 **IF** K$ = "5" **THEN LET** Y = Y-1

      47 **IF** K$ = "8" **THEN LET** Y = Y+1

you can move the cursor all over the screen and draw all kinds of patterns. Moving the cursor horizontally to the left by continually pressing the **5** key will cause the same kind of reflecting from the left boundary as you saw vertically with the **7** key.

There are many enhancements you can make to this program, including:

(1) Use a special character to show the current printing position of the cursor

(2) Allow substitution of different characters for the cursor

(3) Allow erasure of lines

Checking for Input Errors

Whenever you enter data for processing, some items may be invalid. In fact, some of your data may cause the program to stop running. What is even worse, however, is that invalid data will produce erroneous output and go undetected. It is always a good idea to check your data to ensure that it is within an acceptable range. For example, try

PRINT SQR -1

The square root function will return a report code of D because a negative number does not have a real square root. One example of an input check is shown in the program below. First, run it for some positive numbers, then for some negative ones.

```
10 PRINT "NUMBER=?";
20 INPUT N
30 IF N>=0 THEN GOTO 60
40 PRINT "INVALID INPUT"
50 GOTO 10
60 PRINT SQR N
70 GOTO 10
```

Line 30 does the input error check. If the input is greater than or equal to 0, the computer goes on to line 60 and prints the square root. However, if the input is negative, the computer will print the error message to the user and start over again without taking the square root.

A simple **IF** test like the one above works well for one number. But suppose we have two or more numbers to check? The following program shows one case where no error checking is used.

```
10 PRINT "NUMERATOR=?";
20 INPUT N
30 PRINT N
40 PRINT "DENOMINATOR=?";
```

```
50 INPUT D
60 PRINT D
70 LET Q=N/D
80 PRINT "QUOTIENT=";Q
```

This program will print out quotients, Q, unless the denominator =Ø, in which case it will stop with report code/line number 6/7Ø. To prevent this, you can enter error checking lines, as in

```
53 IF D<>Ø THEN GOTO 60
55 PRINT "ERROR-CANNOT BE Ø"
57 GOTO 40
```

Another source of error was discussed in the Number Limits section of Chapter 3. If a result is less than 2.93873588E-39, it is questionable whether it is really correct, since you can't tell if a number is really 2.93873588E-39 or smaller. So, let's put in another check

```
85 IF Q<=2.94E-39 THEN PRINT "QUE
           STIONABLE RESULT"
```

Another possible solution is to set the result of Q to Ø. Instead of 85, you would use

```
75 IF Q<=2.94E-39 THEN LET Q=Ø
```

Let's Be Logical

You have learned how to print numbers by using commands like

```
PRINT 2
```

Now try

	Answer
PRINT 2=2	1
PRINT 2=3	Ø
PRINT 1<2	1
PRINT Ø<=1	1

```
PRINT 5>4                              1
PRINT -3>=-2                           Ø
```

As you've probably guessed, the computer is printing a code to indicate whether the relationship between the two numbers given in each case is true or false. The computer's code is a value of 1 for true and Ø for false.

When you write a condition for an **IF**, the computer will test whether the condition is true or false. For example, try this command:

IF 2=2 **THEN PRINT** "YES"

and you will see YES printed. If the relationship is not true, then nothing will be printed.

In order for you to test relationships easily, such as whether 2=3, enter the following:

```
10 PRINT "RELATION";
20 INPUT R
30 PRINT R
40 GOTO 10
```

As you saw in the section on **INPUT**, the computer can evaluate expressions to give a numerical result.

Try the program above for the following examples, and you will see the same results as in doing a **PRINT** on each relationship.

```
2=2
2=3
1<2
Ø<=1
5>4
-3>=-2
```

The condition for the **IF** is considered true if it does not equal Ø. For example, try the following, where C = 1, 2, 3, -1, -2, and Ø:

```
10 PRINT "CONDITION=?";
20 INPUT C
30 PRINT C
40 IF C THEN GOTO 70
50 PRINT "FALSE"
60 GOTO 10
70 PRINT "TRUE"
80 GOTO 10
```

All of these numbers will print TRUE, except 0, which prints FALSE.

Your computer has some logical operators called **NOT**, **AND**, and **OR**, which help evaluate relationships. Logical operators are analogous to the arithmetic operators, +, -, *, and / for numbers. The logical operators make it easier for you to test relationships.

You can simplify the program above by using the logical operator **NOT**, which is a shifted function under the **N** key. **NOT** is used to give the opposite of a relationship. Try

```
10 INPUT C
20 PRINT C
30 IF C THEN PRINT "TRUE"
40 IF NOT C THEN PRINT "FALSE"
50 GOTO 10
```

In order to see what **NOT** does, try

	Answer
PRINT NOT 0	1
PRINT NOT 1	0

In fact, **NOT** X, where X is any number other than 0, always gives 0.

```
PRINT NOT 2=0
PRINT NOT -1=0
```

So **NOT** gives the opposite of a relationship. It makes true to be false and false to be true.

The **NOT** works on both relationships and expressions. For example, try

	Answer
PRINT NOT 1<2	0
PRINT NOT 3*4-6	0
PRINT NOT 2*2-4	1

AND is another logical operator. Although **NOT** applies to either a single relationship or the expression that follows it, **AND** always needs two relationship or expressions. The **AND** is the shifted **2** key. Try the program

```
10 PRINT "CONDITION=?";
20 INPUT C
30 PRINT C
40 GOTO 10
```

Use as input the following:

Input	Answer
3 **AND** 4	3
3 **AND** 0	0
5 **AND** -1	5
5 **AND** 0	0

The answers show that for two numbers A and B,

A **AND** B gives A if B<>0
A **AND** B gives 0 if B=0

where the <> symbol means *not equal.*

You will find the **AND** operator to be very useful in making certain that a variable stays within a certain range. For example, the statement "X is greater than or equal to A and less than or equal to B," is written as

A< =X< =B

If you are trying to use the **PRINT AT** command to print a symbol or a number at a point on the screen, you would write, mathematically,

$$0 < = X < = 21$$

which is expressed in BASIC as

$$0 < = X \textbf{ AND } X < = 21$$

The statement

$$0 < = Y < = 31$$

is expressed in BASIC as

$$0 < = Y \textbf{ AND } Y < = 31$$

As another example, for the first program in the Months and Days section, we had

```
160 IF N>12 THEN STOP
170 IF N<1 THEN STOP
180 GOTO 10
```

Using **AND**, we can write this in a shorter form:

```
160 IF N>12 AND N<1 THEN GOTO 10
170 STOP
```

Here's another example of using **AND** to save memory. For example, first try the following program without **AND**:

```
10 INPUT X
20 INPUT Y
30 IF X< =Y THEN PRINT "TRUE"
```

and run it using $X = 1$ and $Y = 2$. You will see TRUE printed. Now try it with $X = 5$ and $Y = 0$. Nothing will be printed. The program will just terminate with a report code 0/30. Now change line 30 to

```
30 PRINT "TRUE" AND X< =Y
```

and run the program with the same input as before. You will see the same output, because both versions of line 30 work the same way. However, the **IF** version uses 17 bytes of memory, but the **AND** version uses only 16 bytes. Just remember, you can always trim down your program, if you make every byte count.

We can use **AND** to prevent the reflection problem that we encountered in the Drawing Pictures section. As the cursor moves, we will now stop it when a boundary of the screen is reached—that is, we will move the cursor only when $0<X<21$ and $0<Y<31$. The program from the Drawing Pictures section is shown below with the appropriate changes in lines 40 to 50.

```
10 LET X=11
20 LET Y=16
30 LET K$=INKEY$
40 IF K$="6" AND 0<X AND X<21 THEN LET X=X+1
45 IF K$="5" AND 0<Y AND Y<31 THEN LET Y=Y-1
47 IF K$="8" AND 0<Y AND Y<31 THEN LET Y=Y+1
50 IF K$="7" AND 0<X AND X<21 THEN LET X=X-1
60 PRINT AT X,Y;"*"
70 GOTO 30
```

Assigning the logical test of position to variables is a better way of preventing the reflection problem. This test not only saves memory space and typing, but also speeds up execution.

```
10 LET X=11
20 LET Y=16
30 LET K$=INKEY$
33 LET LX=0<X AND X<21
35 LET LY=0<Y AND Y<31
40 IF K$="6" AND LX THEN LET X=X+1
45 IF K$="5" AND LY THEN LET Y=Y-1
47 IF K$="8" AND LY THEN LET Y=Y+1
50 IF K$="7" AND LX THEN LET X=X-1
```

```
60 PRINT AT X,Y;"*"
70 GOTO 30
```

In the program above, LX is a numeric variable to which the result of the logical test of whether $0<X<21$ is assigned. If $0<X<21$, then $LX=1$, else $LX=0$. Likewise, if $0<Y<31$, then $LY=1$, else $LY=0$.

If line 33 looks strange, try thinking of it with parentheses around the terms, as shown here:

```
33 LET LX=(0<X) AND (X<21)
```

For example, if $X=11$, then

```
0<11 is true
11<21 is true
LX=true AND true
```

so

```
LX=1
```

If you're not sure what a line will do, try it out on the computer. Use a short test program such as

```
100 INPUT X
110 LET LX=(0<X) AND (X<21)
120 PRINT LX
130 GOTO 100
```

This program is put at line numbers higher than your regular program, so that you can have both the test and your program in memory. Try inputting various numbers for X to verify that your program does what you think it should. Experiment with your computer.

You will notice that LX and LY can only have a value of 0 or 1. Therefore, you should consider LX and LY to be logical variables rather than numeric variables. In some computer languages, such as Pascal, FORTRAN, and C, a distinction is made between logical and other types of variables. BASIC, however, does not provide for a separate variable type.

When it is in operation, the computer evaluates the relationships first (see line 40), such as

    K$ = "6"

If this is true and LX is true, then X = X + 1. Likewise, the other lines 45, 47, and 50 are tested before the "*" is printed in line 60. An even shorter version is

```
10 LET X=11
20 LET Y=16
30 LET K$=INKEY$
40 LET X=X+(K$="6")-(K$="7")
50 LET Y=Y+(K$="8")-(K$="5")
60 PRINT AT X,Y;"*"
70 GOTO 30
```

Suppose K$ = "6" is true, then K$ = "5" is false. Line 40 gives

    LET X = X + 1-0 = X + 1

Likewise, if K$ = "5" is true, then line 40 gives

    LET X = X + 0-1 = X-1

The same effects occur for Y in line 50.

OR, the last logical operator of BASIC, checks to determine if one condition *or* another is true. It is a shifted **W** key. Try the following:

	Answer
PRINT 3 **OR** 4	1
PRINT 3 **OR** 0	3
PRINT 5 **OR** -1	1
PRINT 5 **OR** 0	5

Like **AND, OR** needs two numbers on which to operate. For two numbers A and B,

A **OR** B gives A if B=0

A **OR** B gives 1 if B<>0

OR's usefulness is demonstrated in the version of the program to print the days of the month, shown below. Compare this program to the one in the Months and Days section of this chapter.

```
10 PRINT "ENTER MONTH";

20 INPUT M$

30 PRINT M$

40 IF M$="JANUARY" OR
M$="MARCH" OR M$="MAY" OR M$="JULY" OR
M$="AUGUST" OR M$="OCTOBER" OR
M$="DECEMBER" THEN PRINT 31

50 IF M$="APRIL" OR M$="JUNE" OR
M$="NOVEMBER" OR M$="SEPTEMBER" THEN
PRINT 30

60 IF M$="FEBRUARY" THEN PRINT 28

70 GOTO 10
```

Note that while you're entering lines 40 and 50, just keep typing without pressing **ENTER** until all the characters are in. The computer will keep adding to the line you're entering. The program in the Months and Days section uses 16 lines, but the **OR** program above uses only 7 lines.

As shown in Appendix B, **NOT** has priority over **AND**, and **AND** has priority over **OR**. All of these commands have less priority than arithmetic operators. For example,

PRINT NOT 1-1

gives 1 because the 1-1 is done first to give 0 and then **NOT** 0=1. However, if **NOT** had equal or higher priority, it would have been **NOT** 1=0, and then **PRINT** 0-1 would have given -1. When in doubt about priorities, just test the commands on the computer.

Being Friendly to Strangers

The Months and Days program can be modified to help children learn to spell the names of the months. For example,

```
  5 REM MONTH SPELLING DRILL
 10 PRINT "HI, WHAT IS YOUR NAME?";
 20 INPUT N$
 30 PRINT N$
 40 LET T$ = ", TRY ANOTHER"
 50 LET M = INT (12*RND + 1)
 60 PRINT "SPELL MONTH";M;",";N$
 70 INPUT M$
 80 IF M$ = "END" THEN STOP
 90 IF M$ = "JANUARY" AND M = 1 THEN GOTO 230
100 IF M$ = "FEBRUARY" AND M = 2 THEN GOTO 230
110 IF M$ = "MARCH" AND M = 3 THEN GOTO 230
120 IF M$ = "APRIL" AND M = 4 THEN GOTO 230
130 IF M$ = "MAY" AND M = 5 THEN GOTO 230
140 IF M$ = "JUNE" AND M = 6 THEN GOTO 230
150 IF M$ = "JULY" AND M = 7 THEN GOTO 230
160 IF M$ = "AUGUST" AND M = 8 THEN GOTO 230
170 IF M$ = "SEPTEMBER" AND M = 9 THEN GOTO 230
180 IF M$ = "OCTOBER" AND M = 10 THEN GOTO 230
190 IF M$ = "NOVEMBER" AND M = 11 THEN GOTO 230
200 IF M$ = "DECEMBER" AND M = 12 THEN GOTO 230
210 PRINT "SORRY,";N$;T$
220 GOTO 50
230 PRINT "YOU ARE RIGHT,";N$;T$
240 GOTO 50
```

This program has some interesting features. In line 10, the program asks the child's name and then stores it in the string variable

N$. In printing messages, the program will address the child by name. This is a feature of a user-friendly program, one that is designed to make the user feel comfortable.

Although nobody tries to write a user-*un*friendly program, many programs are written for more experienced users, for whom brief messages are used. Longer messages are more informative to an inexperienced user, but they do take more time to print out and need more storage space in memory.

In line 4Ø, the string ",TRY ANOTHER" is stored as the string variable T$. Except for the initial attempt, this phrase is used every time the child tries to spell a month. In terms of memory storage, the variable T$ takes up about half the space used by the string ",TRY ANOTHER." If this phrase were likely to be used many times, you would definitely save memory by using the string variable instead of the string. This maneuver is analogous to saving storage by using a numeric variable instead of a constant. Using a string variable also involves less typing for you.

Line 5Ø generates a random number from 1 to 12 and stores it in the variable M$. A random number greater than or equal to Ø, but less than 12, is generated by 12***RND**. By adding .5 and applying the **INT** function, we get a whole number M from 1 to 12.

Line 6Ø prints output like

      SPELL MONTH 2,JOE

Line 7Ø stores the input in the string M$.

Line 8Ø is put in so that the user can type END to stop the program. Or another possibility is to include a line of explanation, such as

      35 **PRINT** "TYPE END TO STOP THE PROGRAM"

or

      6Ø **PRINT** "SPELL MONTH. TYPE END TO STOP"
      ;M;",";N$

or you could enter **STOP** to stop in line 6Ø.

The **IF** test is used in lines 90 to 200 to see if M$ matches a month. If M$ matches, the computer will go to line 230 and print out the message

    YOU ARE RIGHT,JOE,TRY ANOTHER

and then loop back to line 50 to generate another random number.

If every **IF** test fails in lines 90 to 200, because the child has not spelled any month correctly, the computer will execute line 210. This line prints out as

    SORRY,JOE,TRY ANOTHER

Then the program returns to line 50.

You can improve the appearance of your output by scrolling the display, instead of printing directly. Without scrolling, the screen will fill up and the program will stop. An inexperienced user may not know to press **CONT** to continue when the screen is full.

Since the month numbers are generated randomly in your program, you may get the same month number several times in a row. You can get rid of this annoying problem by storing the previous value of M and comparing it to the new value. You would only use the new value as the month number if it differs from the old value. If the number is the same, the program will keep generating random numbers until a different one is found.

Is Your Leap Okay?

Logical operators can be used in programs to determine the number of days between two dates. Your program must always allow for the extra day in a leap year. Many people think that any year divisible by 4 is a leap year. That is generally true for most years. But the exact rule is: if the year is also exactly divisible by 100 (has no remainder), it is not a leap year unless it is also exactly divisible by 400. For example,

Year	Leap Year
1600	Yes
1601	No
1602	No
1603	No
1604	Yes
1700	No
1800	No
1900	No
1980	Yes
1984	Yes
2000	yes

Again, you can see from these examples that the following rules apply:

Rule 1: If the year is exactly divisible by 4 and not by 100, then it is a leap year. This covers 1604, 1980, 1984.

Rule 2: If the year is exactly divisible by 400, then it is a leap year. This covers years 1600, 2000, etc.

Any other year is not a leap year. Therefore, a year is a leap year if it satisfies rule 1 or rule 2.

How can you tell if a year is exactly divisible by a particular number? One way is to determine if the remainder, after division, is 0. For example, try

Example	Answer
PRINT 1980/4	495

but

Example	Answer
PRINT 1981/4	495.25
PRINT 1982/4	495.5
PRINT 1983/4	495.75

As you can see, only 1980 has no remainder and is exactly divisible by 4.

If you apply the Integer Function to a number, you get the integer part. For example,

Example	Answer
PRINT INT(1980/4)	495
PRINT INT(1981/4)	495
PRINT INT(1982/4)	495
PRINT INT(1983/4)	495

For our examples, then,

Example	Answer	Meaning
PRINT 1980/4=**INT**(1980/4)	1	True
PRINT 1981/4=**INT**(1981/4)	0	False
PRINT 1982/4=**INT**(1982/4)	0	False
PRINT 1983/4=**INT**(1983/4)	0	False

And we can express the first part of rule 1 as the test

$$Y/4 = INT(Y/4)$$

in which Y stands for year.

The second part of rule 1 can be written as

NOT Y/100=**INT**(Y/100)

We don't have to put parentheses around the Y/100 =**INT**(Y/100), because the = operator has higher precedence than **NOT** (see Appendix B) and is, therefore, evaluated first. For example, try

	Answer	Meaning
PRINT 1900/100=**INT**(1900/100)	1	True

Here, **NOT** true=false, and 1900 is not a leap year by this test. In fact, any year divisible by 100 fails this test, which is why we need rule 2.

We can now write the test of rule 1 as

$$Y/4 = INT(Y/4) \textbf{ AND NOT } Y/100 = INT(Y/100)$$

and the test of rule 2 as

$$Y/400 = \mathbf{INT}(Y/400)$$

If rule 1 or rule 2 is true, we have a leap year. Thus our combined rule is

$$Y/4 = \mathbf{INT}(Y/4) \textbf{ AND NOT } Y/100 = \mathbf{INT}(Y/100) \textbf{ OR}$$
$$Y/400 = \mathbf{INT}(Y/400)$$

We don't need parentheses around the terms, because, by operator priority, everything works out.

The following program shows how a check is made for a leap year:

```
 5 REM LEAP YEAR CHECK
10 PRINT "YEAR=?";
20 INPUT Y
30 PRINT Y
40 IF Y/4=INT(Y/4) AND NOT Y/100=INT(Y/100) OR
   Y/400=INT(Y/400) THEN GOTO 70
60 GOTO 10
70 PRINT "YES, LEAP YEAR"
80 GOTO 10
```

Enter and run this program for the years discussed above, and you will see that line 40 works correctly.

CHAPTER 11
Doing Loops

There will be times when you want the computer to repeat calculations. When the computer does this, it is said to be looping. In this chapter, we'll see a number of ways to do loops. We'll also see the advantages and disadvantages of different ways of making loops.

Tables and Squares

Suppose you want to print a table showing the squares of the numbers from 1 to 10. Enter and run the following:

```
 5 REM TABLE OF SQUARES
10 LET C=1
20 PRINT "NUMBER";TAB 10;"SQUARE"
30 PRINT C;TAB 10;C*C
40 LET C=C+1
50 IF C=11 THEN STOP
60 GOTO 30
```

A table of numbers and their squares will be printed.

```
NUMBER     SQUARE
1          1
2          4
3          9
4          16
5          25
6          36
7          49
8          64
9          81
1Ø         1ØØ
```

Now try this program in **FAST** mode. You can see how much faster it is than **SLOW** mode, even though the screen goes blank in **FAST** while all the calculations are being done. Now return to **SLOW** mode.

Is there any way to shorten this program? Try replacing lines 5Ø and 6Ø with

      5Ø **GOTO** 3Ø **AND** C$<$11

and running it.

At first, this version of the program seems to work well, and it does print out the table. Unfortunately, it never stops. It keeps printing out table after table. Line 5Ø gives a value of 3Ø if C$<$11. However, when C$=$11, we have

      5Ø **GOTO** Ø

since 3Ø **AND** False gives a Ø. This command sends the computer back to the first line of your program, creating a situation in which execution never stops. The program is said to be *caught* or *trapped in a loop.*

The Easy Way

You can set up a controlled loop with the BASIC commands **FOR**, **TO**, and **NEXT**. **FOR** is a keyword located over the **F** key, **TO** is over the **4** key, and **NEXT** is over the **N** key. Try this version of the Squares program:

```
 5 REM TABLE OF SQUARES
10 PRINT "NUMBER";TAB 10;"SQUARE"
20 FOR C=1 TO 10
30 PRINT C;TAB 10;C*C
40 NEXT C
```

and you will see the table of squares printed out. Notice that we've used only 4 lines in this version as compared to the 6 lines in the first version.

The variable named C in line 20 is called the *index variable* of the loop. In T/S 1000 BASIC, the index variable must have a name consisting of a single letter from A to Z.

The amount the index variable is changed is called the *step size*, which can be either positive or negative. **STEP** is the **E** key shifted.

Lines 20 and 40 of the Squares program set up a **FOR-NEXT** loop. The computer executes the lines down to the **NEXT**, loops back to the line following **FOR**, then repeats this sequence until the loop is done.

The number preceding the **TO** in line 20 is called the *lower limit*. The number following it is called the *upper limit*, or just *limit*. The index variable is set-initially to the value of the lower limit. Then the lines following the **FOR** statement are executed until the **NEXT** statement. In the Table of Squares example, the index variable is then incremented by 1 and checked against the upper limit. If the index variable exceeds the upper limit, the loop is ended, and the line following the **NEXT** is executed. If the index variable is less than or equal to the upper limit, the computer executes the line following the **FOR** statement, called the looping line.

The program lines between **FOR** and **NEXT** are called the *body* of the loop. You can have as many lines in the body of a loop as the memory capacity of your computer permits.

To see what a negative step size will do in your program, change line 20 to

        20 **FOR** C=10 **TO** 1 **STEP** -1

and you will see the Square table printed in reverse order.

        NUMBER   SQUARE
        10   100
        9   81
        8   64
        7   49
        6   36
        5   25
        4   16
        3   9
        2   4
        1   1

Unless specified otherwise the value of **STEP** is 1. Therefore,

        FOR C=1 **TO** 10 **STEP** 1

is the same as

        FOR C=1 **TO** 10

You can also **STEP** in noninteger values. For example, change line 20 to

        20 **FOR** C=1 **TO** 10 **STEP** .5

Now you will see

        NUMBER   SQUARE
        1   1
        1.5   2.25
        2   4
        2.5   6.25
        3   9
        3.5   12.25
        4   16
        4.5   20.25

5	25
5.5	30.25
6	36
6.5	42.25
7	49
7.5	56.25
8	64
8.5	72.25
9	81
9.5	90.25
10	100

How to Make Your Computer Lie

Let's try an even smaller step size. Change line 20 to

20 FOR C = 1 **TO** 10 **STEP** .1

and run it. When the screen gets full and execution stops, press **CONT** to continue. You may also want to switch to **FAST** mode to avoid watching each line get printed.

If you look at the last line of output, you will see something peculiar. Instead of

10	100

you will see

9.9	98.1

Why did the computer stop outputting before C = 10? If you look at the report code, you will see a 0, showing that the computer thinks it is done. Since the computer should stop when C = 10, let's print out C. Try

PRINT C

and you will get 10 as the result.

This is a lie. The value of C is not exactly 10: it is about 10.

To show C with more precision, enter

PRINT C-1Ø

A value of

.45Ø58Ø6E-9

will appear on the display. Thus, C is actually about

1Ø.ØØØØØØØØØ45Ø58Ø6

rather than the integer 1Ø.

The loop stopped as it should, because C exceeded the upper limit of the loop. Now try

PRINT 1Ø.ØØØØØØØØØ45Ø58Ø6

A 1Ø will be printed on the display. The **PRINT** rounds off answers to 9 digits, therefore, it printed 1Ø.ØØØØØØØØØ45Ø58Ø6 as 1Ø.

The reason why C was not exactly 1Ø is that numbers are only stored and calculated to a certain precision in the computer. As a result, errors may build up. (See Chapter 3.)

What's inside Your Computer

The computer actually operates and stores *binary numbers.* The term "bi" is from the Latin and means *two.* In the binary system, only the numerals Ø and 1 are used. In our familiar decimal system, we use the digits Ø, 1, 2, 3, 4, 5, 6, 7, 8, and 9. In fact, the word digit means "1Ø."

The following table shows the binary and decimal equivalents.

Binary Number	Decimal Number
Ø	Ø
1	1
1Ø	2
11	3
1ØØ	4
1Ø1	5

110	6
111	7
1000	8
1001	9
1010	10
1011	11
1100	12
1101	13
1110	14
1111	15
10000	16

The computer's working parts are made up of tiny electronic circuits called *integrated circuits* (ICs). There are four ICs in your T/S 1000. One IC contains the memory. The memory IC contains a small quarter-inch square chip of silicon. This is the actual IC, also called a *chip*. Surrounding the IC is the case. The IC is composed of small circuits that process and store binary data. Each 0 or 1 is called a *binary digit,* or *bit*. A *byte* is composed of 8 bits, the basic group that the Z80 central processor unit (CPU) can process. The Z80 is also called a *microprocessor* because it is a central processor unit on a chip. Large computers usually have a CPU composed of many chips. Although this increases their speed, it also increases their cost. Other microprocessors, such as the Intel 8086, can handle 16 bits at a time.

Number Precision

Different computer designs use different amounts of memory to store data. For example, in the T/S 1000, the value of a number is stored as 5 bytes, or 40 bits. The technique used to convert a decimal number to a binary number of 40 bits permits a precision of about 9 1/2 decimal digits.

Since a number is stored in binary, it is stored accurately if it is an integer of a power of 2.

For example,

$$16 = 2^4 = 10000$$
$$8 = 2^3 = 1000$$
$$4 = 2^2 = 100$$
$$2 = 2^1 = 10$$
$$1 = 2^0 = 1$$
$$.5 = 2^{-1} = .1$$
$$.25 = 2^{-2} = .11$$
$$.125 = 2^{-3} = .111$$
$$.0625 = 2^{-4} = .1111$$

Some decimal numbers can be stored exactly in binary, but others can't. This is like the case of 1/3, which can only be expressed approximately, as a decimal fraction.

$$1/3 = .33333333....$$

If you use 10, 20, or even a 100 terms of the decimal equivalent, you will still get only an approximation of 1/3. In the same way, the computer can only store an approximation of a number, which may or may not be exact. A particularly bad number is the decimal 0.1. When the step size is .1, the computer can use only its binary approximation of 0.1. Every time it goes through the loop, the computer adds its approximation of 0.1 to the current value of the index variable. As a result, the index variable becomes increasingly inaccurate as approximations are being added to approximations. Finally, after 100 additions of the step size to the starting index value, the computer gets

$$C = 10.0000000004505806$$

instead of exactly 10. Since this value of C exceeds the upper limit, the **FOR-NEXT** loop is ended. You can't see the inaccuracy in printing C after the loop is over, because the **PRINT** command of BASIC only prints out 8 digits for calculations.

All about Squares

As a final example illustrating the binary nature of the computer, let's find all the numbers from 1 to 100 that have an integer square root. In other words,

1 has the integer square root 1 since 1*1=1

4 has the integer square root 2 since 2*2=4

9 has the integer square root 3 since 3*3=9

and so on. The other numbers are 16, 25, 36, 49, 64, and 81. Some numbers have a square root that is not an integer. For example, the square root of 17 is 4.1231056.

There are two ways to solve this problem. The easiest is to write a program like

```
10 FOR I=1 TO 50
20 IF I*I>100 THEN STOP
30 PRINT I;TAB 5;I*I
40 NEXT I
```

where the upper limit is set to 50, because we'll assume we don't know the highest number. If you run this program, you will get the integers 1, 2, 3, 4, 5, 6, 7, 8, 9, and 10 as well as their squares.

Now let's try it the hard way and really exercise the **SQR** and **INT** functions of your computer. Try

```
10 FOR I=1 TO 100
20 PRINT I
30 IF SQR I=INT SQR I THEN PRINT "YES"
40 NEXT I
```

Line 20 prints the number being tested. Line 30 checks to ensure that the square root of the number being tested is an integer. The **INT** function can only return an integer. For example,

SQR 4=2=**INT SQR** 4

But

SQR 5=2.236068 is unequal to **INT SQR** 5=2

When you run this program, the first screenful of output will be

```
1

YES

2

3

4

YES

5

6

7

8

9

YES

10

11

12

13

14

15

16

YES

17

18
```

So far, so good. To show the next screenful, press **CONT**. If you want to speed things up, go to **FAST** mode.

When you print the second screenful of output, you will see a problem. A "YES" is not printed after 25 or 36. Yet, each of these numbers has an integer root. If you continue, you will see a "YES" after 64. But, a "YES" will not be printed after 80 or 100.

Let's Debug

To debug this program, let's find out what results the computer calculates for the **SQR** and **INT SQR** of numbers. Entering this test program will help us debug our square root program.

```
10 PRINT "NUMBER=?";
20 INPUT I
30 PRINT I
40 PRINT "SQR=";SQR I
50 PRINT "INT SQR=";INT SQR I
60 PRINT "SQR-INT SQR=";SQR I-INT SQR I
70 GOTO 10
```

This program will print out the square root, its integer part, and the difference between the square root and the integer part. The difference, calculated in line 50, is important, because it is what the **IF** test in line 30 of the square root program is checking. If the difference = 0, then **SQR I=INT SQR**, and the computer prints "YES."

Run this program for 1, and you will see

```
NUMBER=?1
SQR=1
INT SQR=1
SQR-INT SQR=0
```

A "YES" will be printed.

Now try the number 16.

```
NUMBER=?16
SQR=4
INT SQR=4
SQR-INT SQR=0
```

Again, a "YES" is printed.

Now try 24.

        NUMBER = ?24
        SQR = 4.8989795
        INT SQR = 4
        SQR-INT SQR = 0.89897949

The SQR 24-INT SQR 24 is not 0, therefore the **IF** test fails, and no "YES" is printed.

Try 25, and you will see

        NUMBER = 25
        SQR = 5
        INT SQR = 5
        SQR-INT SQR = 1.8626452E-9

No "YES" was printed, because SQR 25 is not equal to INT SQR 25 by 1.8626452E-9. This small a value is not printed by **PRINT**, because it only prints the 8 most significant digits of calculations. You can also get this result by

        PRINT SQR 25-5

which means that the value of **SQR** 25 is returned as 5.0000000018626452 rather than 5.

If you try 49, 81, and 100, you will see that the difference between **SQR** and **INT SQR** is not exactly 0, because the **SQR** does not return an exact answer. However, 64 gives

        NUMBER = 64
        SQR = 8
        INT SQR = 8
        SQR-INT SQR = 0

and the **IF** from line 30 of the square program prints "YES." Notice that

        64 = 8*8 = 2*2*2*2*2*2

You can also write this equation using powers. Since there are six 2's, we can write

$$64 = 2^6$$

64 is a power of 2.

To Tell the Truth

The computer is a binary machine; therefore, it can store powers of 2 exactly. That's why the square root of 64 was calculated exactly in the example above.

The next highest power of 2 having an integer square root is $2^8 = 256$. Try 256 in your program, and you will also get a difference of 0. Other numbers, such as $144 = 12^2$ and $169 = 13^2$ won't give a zero difference. As another test, try 4096, which is 2^{12} in your program, and it will still give you an exact answer. The computer always tells the truth, if you use a number that is a power of 2.

These examples were designed to show you that the computer is really a binary machine. Although electronic circuits that operate with the decimal system have been constructed, they were more costly, slower, and more complex than binary circuits. In fact, some of the first computers were decimal machines, but they could not compete effectively with the binary computers.

Today, software is used to manage the decimal-to-binary conversion when you input, and binary-to-decimal conversion when the computer outputs. In a hand calculator, the software for these conversions is built-in so that it operates like a decimal machine. Its slow speed is not a problem, because you are entering all data by hand, which takes a while. Also, a simple hand calculator has no way of doing loops, which would also show the calculator's slow speed. You can do 64.1-64 on a calculator and get a 0.1. Computers, on the other hand, are optimized for speed of operation, so decimal operation is not built-in. On the computer, however, **PRINT** 64.1-64 does not give .1.

A Word by Any Other Name

When you entered the line

60 **PRINT** "SQR-INT SQR";**SQR** I-**INT SQR** I

in your debugging program, did you type in each character of **SQR** and **INT** between the quotation marks? Instead, you could have used the BASIC tokens **SQR** and **INT**. The term *token* is the computer term for the smallest unit of meaning to the computer. You can save memory space by using tokens instead of characters. Keywords, such as **PRINT**, **PAUSE**, and **RUN**, are converted to a one byte code, or token, for the computer. The operators and symbols *, **, $<=$, $<>$, +, -, $>=$, $>$, and $<$ are also converted to tokens. That's why you can't press the N key for $<$, and **M** key for $>$ to make $<>$. You have to press the **T** key to generate the single code for $<>$.

In line 60, you can use the BASIC tokens for the words between the quotation marks. For example, enter

60 **PRINT** "

and then press **SHIFT** and **ENTER**, and then the **H** key. You will see **SQR** appear, since you've input the BASIC token for **SQR**. The token **SQR** is stored the same as the function **SQR**, except that it is not evaluated. Although the token **SQR** appears to you as 3 characters, S, Q, and R, it is actually stored inside the computer as a single byte. The word SQR is therefore not the same as the token **SQR**. They are just printed the same way.

You can save memory space by using the 1 byte token to store **SQR** instead of using 3 bytes to store the function **SQR**. Try using other functions such as

PRINT " STOP THEN RUN "

or mix up characters with tokens.

PRINT "NOT AT HOME"

You can also use the red shifted keys, except **EDIT,** arrow keys, **GRAPHICS, DELETE, ", FUNCTION,** and **SHIFT.** Try

> **PRINT "AND THEN TO OR $< = <>$"**

and other commands, using tokens instead of spelling out the words or operators.

The keyword over each key can also be used to save space. The trick is to use **THEN** followed by the keyword. The **THEN** token puts the computer into a state where it thinks that the next keypress will be a keyword, not the letter on the key. For example, try

> **10 PRINT "**

then press the **SHIFT** and **3** and you will get

> **10 PRINT " THEN**

Now you can enter any keyword, because BASIC expects a keyword after a **THEN.** Press the **R** key and you will see

> **10 PRINT " THEN RUN**

Now **SHIFT** and press the **2** key, and you will get

> **10 PRINT " THEN RUN AND**

Suppose you want to add the word SAVE. If you press the **S** key, you will get an S, because only one keyword can follow **THEN.** To get the keyword **SAVE,** you have to enter another **THEN** token. Press **SHIFT** and **3** to enter **THEN,** then press the **S** key. Add another quotation mark and you've got

> **10 PRINT " THEN RUN AND THEN SAVE "**

This line is fine if it contains the message you want. But suppose the message you want is **"RUN AND SAVE."** Simply go into **EDIT** mode to delete the two **THEN** tokens. Press **SHIFT** and the **1** key to edit line 10. Then press the **SHIFT** and the **8** key to advance the cursor to just beyond the first **THEN.** Press **SHIFT** and the **0** key to delete it. Now move the cursor just beyond the second **THEN** and delete it also.

This technique may seem like a lot of work, but it does save code. In our example, only 3 bytes are used for **"RUN AND SAVE"** as opposed to the 12 bytes that would have been used if each letter and space were spelled out.

Setting Limits

Regular numeric variable names can be used for the lower limit, upper limit, and step size of a **FOR** statement. Only the *index variable,* the variable that follows **NEXT,** must be a single letter. For example, enter

```
10 LET LL=-3
20 LET UL=6
30 LET ST=2
40 FOR I=LL TO UL STEP ST
50 PRINT I,I*I
60 NEXT I
```

and you will see

-3	9
-1	1
1	1
3	9
5	25

You can also allow expressions in the **FOR** statement. Try replacing line 40 with

```
40 FOR I=LL+1 TO 2*UL-2 STEP ST/2
```

and running it. The output will be the same as if you used

```
40 FOR I=-2 TO 10 STEP 1
```

because the arithmetic expressions are evaluated by the computer to obtain the lower limit, upper limit, and step size. The output is shown below for either version.

-2	4
-1	1
0	0
1	1
2	4
3	9
4	16
5	25
6	36
7	49
8	64
9	81
10	100

Abused Loops

Let's take a closer look at loop limits to see how they can be abused.

```
 5 REM LOOP TEST
10 PRINT "L=?";
20 INPUT L
30 PRINT L
40 PRINT "U=?";
50 INPUT U
60 PRINT U
70 PRINT "STEP=?";
80 INPUT S
90 PRINT S
100 FOR I=L TO U STEP S
110 PRINT I
```

```
120 NEXT I
130 PRINT "DONE:I=";I
```

If you run this program for L=1, U=3, and S=1, you will see the following output:

```
1
2
3
DONE:I=4
```

Now try it for L=5 and U=4, and you will get

```
DONE:I=5
```

since the body of the loop is not executed.

Try this program using other upper limits that are less than the lower limit. The result is always the same. The body of the loop is not executed, and the control variable is set to the lower limit.

Now let's look at a negative limit. Try L=-3, U=1, and S=1 in your program, and you will get

```
-3
-2
-1
0
1
DONE:I=2
```

For a positive size, the loop executes until the step size plus the current value of the control variable exceeds the upper limit. Now try L=3, U=1, and S=-1 in your program, and you will get

```
3
2
1
DONE: I=0
```

For a negative step size, the loop executes until the current value of the control variable plus the step size is less than the upper limit.

What happens when there is an error? Try L=-3, U=1, and S=-1 in your program.

In this case, you might think that the loop would never end, since the current value plus the step size gets further from the upper limit.

Instead, we see

    DONE: I=-3

Your computer is smart enough to recognize that the loop parameters it was given would lead it into an endless loop, and so it avoids the situation.

The Times of Their Loops
OR
Doing Nothing May Be Useful

Loops are useful for timing. As you've seen, the problem with using **PAUSE** is that it introduces a flicker on the screen. Also, you can only use **PAUSE** to time in increments of 1/60 of a second. You can achieve better resolution with loops.

To show this, enter the following program:

```
 5 REM LOOP TEST
10 PRINT "U=?";
20 INPUT U
30 FOR I=1 TO U
40 NEXT I
50 PRINT "DONE"
```

Now the loop

```
30 FOR I=1 TO U
```

40 **NEXT** I

will start executing immediately after you enter U. Nothing will be output until it is done, so the computer will execute at maximum speed.

Now let's see how fast your computer can count to 10. Try U = 10, and then U = 100. Even this is too fast to time accurately a single loop, so try U = 1000. The execution will take about 28 seconds in **SLOW** mode, but about 5 seconds in **FAST** mode.
In **SLOW** mode, a loop executes in 28/1000 = .028 seconds per single loop, which is longer than the 1/60 = .0167 seconds of **PAUSE**. However, if you try U = 10000 in **FAST**, you will get about 45 seconds or 45/10000 = .0045 seconds per single loop. You still get the flicker in **FAST** mode, but the minimum timing resolution is much less than in **PAUSE**.

A loop that performs no calculations—nothing—can still do something useful if it is used for timing. In particular, if you're designing a game or other program with visual prompts, a **SLOW** loop works well because there is no flicker.

Nom de Plume

What happens if you try to change the value of the limits in the body of the loop? Let's try it and see. Enter

35 **IF** I = 5 **THEN LET** UL = 9

and run the program. You will see the same numbers printed out as before. If line 35 had changed UL where I = 9, then the numbers 6, 7, and 8 would not be printed. However, if you print UL after the loop terminates, you will see that it does equal 9.

Why doesn't the loop terminate when I = 5? When the computer encounters the **FOR** loop for the first time, it evaluates the expressions for lower limit, upper limit, and step size. It stores these loop parameters and the looping line right after the control variable in the variable area. The computer checks the value of the control variable against the upper limit each time the **NEXT** statement is executed. The computer then uses their values to decide when the loop is done. A *parameter* is a number that affects or controls something else. You can think of these parameters as being written under a different name in the computer's memory.

Basically, the computer uses a *nom de plume* (pen name), or pseudonym (false name) for the loop parameters. When the **FOR** statement is first executed, it sets up the control variable and loop parameters in the variable area. You can't change the parameters in the variable area with a **LET** statement. When you change the lower limit, upper limit, and step size in the body of the loop, you're not affecting the loop parameters because you're not writing to the nom de plume. Evaluating and storing parameters reduces execution time, because the expressions don't have to be evaluated each time the computer goes through the loop.

However, you can change the control variable inside the body of the loop. For example, try

```
10 FOR I=1 TO 10
20 PRINT I
30 IF I=5 THEN LET I=9
40 NEXT I
```

When you run this, you will see

```
1
2
3
4
5
10
```

When I was changed to 9 by line 30, its value was incremented by 1 in line 40, and then printed as 10 by line 20.

What is the final value of I? Try a **PRINT** I, and you will see that I=11 after the loop is done. Line 40 is equivalent to

```
LET I=I+1
```

IF I>1Ø **THEN GOTO** 2Ø

In general, the final value of the control variable is equal to the upper limit plus the step size.

Birds Do It

What do birds and loops have in common? Answer: both can make nests. The term *nested loops* is used to describe loops that occur entirely within another loop. If loops do not, then they are illegal.

Try this example

```
10 FOR I=0 TO 3
20 FOR J=1 TO 7
30 PRINT 7*I+J;
40 NEXT J
50 NEXT I
```

and you will see the digits 123...28 being output on the screen. Let's look at how this program works.

The computer first executes line 1Ø, which sets I=Ø. Then it executes line 2Ø, which sets J=1. Next, line 3Ø prints a 1 on the screen, since

$$7*\emptyset+1=1$$

Now the computer executes line 4Ø, which increments J by 1, so J=2. Since 2 is less than the upper limit of 7 for J, the computer loops back to line 3Ø and prints 2, because

$$7*\emptyset+2=2$$

The computer executes line 4Ø next and increases 2 to 3. Since 3 is still less than 7, it goes back to line 3Ø and prints 3, because

$$7*\emptyset+3=3$$

The computer keeps looping back to line 30 and printing 4, 5, 6, and finally 7 on the screen.

Now J=8 from line 40, so the computer doesn't go back to line 30. Instead, it goes to the next line after 40, which is line 50, and increases I to 1. Since I=1 is less than its upper limit of 3, the computer goes to line 20 and sets up the J loop again. Starting with J=1, line 30 now does this:

PRINT 7*1+1

or 8. Then the computer increments J to 2, loops back to line 30, and prints 9, since

7*1+2=9

on the screen. By now you should be getting a clear idea of how the process works. After J=8 again, I is set to 2 in line 50, and we go back to line 20 and set up the J loop again. Now, the computer prints out

Output	Calculation from Line 30
15	7*2+1=15
16	7*2+2=16
..	....
..	....
21	7*2+7=21

Then I is set to 3 in line 50, and the computer loops back to line 20, where J=1, and prints

7*3+1=22

7*3+2=23

....

7*3+7=28

At this point, you may be thinking that we could have accomplished the same thing by using a single loop, such as

FOR J=1 **TO** 28

There is a reason for setting up two nested loops like this, which we will consider below.

Printing a Month

Change line 30 to

    30 **PRINT** 7*I + J;**TAB**(4*J);

Then add

    45 **PRINT**

and run again. Now you will see the output spaced in four rows of seven columns, rather like a calendar for the month of February.

1	2	3	4	5	6	7
8	9	10	11	12	13	14
15	16	17	18	19	20	21
22	23	24	25	26	27	28

The inner J loop prints the 7 days of the week, while the outer I loop prints the four weeks of the month. By setting up two nested loops, you can print out a rectangular pattern of data.

In line 30, we've added a **TAB** that spaces over 4 columns every time J is incremented. Notice that there is a semicolon after the **TAB** to keep the 7 numbers on the same row. The **PRINT** in line 45 is added to start printing on the next row by stopping printing on a line after seven numbers are printed.

If, in this illustration, Sunday is on the first day of the month, you can make your output look even more like a calendar by adding the line

    5 **PRINT** "SUN MON TUE WED THU FRI SAT"

To demonstrate how this program can be used to print out a month, given the first day, let's rewrite it as follows:

    5 **REM** PRINT A MONTH GIVEN THE FIRST WEEKDAY
    10 **LET** COL = 4

```
20 PRINT "DAYS IN MONTH?"
30 INPUT DM
40 PRINT DM
50 PRINT "FIRST WEEKDAY?-SUN=0";
60 INPUT W
70 PRINT W
80 PRINT "SUN MON TUE WED THU FRI SAT"
90 LET CUR=1
100 FOR I=0 TO 5
110 FOR J=1 TO 7
120 PRINT TAB 4*W;CUR;
130 IF CUR=DM THEN STOP
140 LET CUR=CUR+1
150 IF W=6 THEN GOTO 180
160 LET W=W+1
170 NEXT J
180 LET W=0
190 PRINT
200 NEXT I
```

This program prints a calendar month on the screen. Input the number of days in the month, DM, in line 20. Then input the first weekday of the month, where

```
SUN= 0
MON=1
TUE= 2
WED=3
THU= 4
FRI=  5
SAT= 6
```

For example, October, 1982, began on a Friday, so enter 5 in response to the "FIRST WEEKDAY?-SUN=0" prompt from the computer. In a later program, we'll show you how the computer can calculate the starting day of any month. Right now, we're just showing a program to print the month in the way we want. This is called *formatting* the output. The term *format* means the order in which items are arranged. This program will be combined with another to print a calendar for any month.

Rather than trying to develop a big program all at once, it is better to develop and test smaller portions, called *modules*. These modules may then be combined to form larger programs. In fact, this concept is part of the foundation of *structured programming*. A large program is broken up into small modules, which are developed and tested independently, perhaps by more than one programmer. When the programmers are sure each module works correctly, the modules are combined with others to form the larger program. Right now, we've developed a module to print output for a month, once we know what day of the week the first day of the month occurs. Notice how this module is tested as a separate program. When we're sure this code works correctly, it can be used in any program.

Line 70 prints a header showing the three-letter abbreviations for the days of the week. If you have a printer that prints more than 32 columns, you can change this line to print the complete names of the days.

Line 80 initializes a variable that prints the current date, CUR, to the first day of the month. Line 90 starts the loop to print the weeks. With up to 31 days in a month, the days may spread out over six weeks. The weeks are numbered from 0 to 5 to simplify calculating the date for each day. Line 120 provides the column spacing, COL = 4, and prints the current date after tabbing over 4 spaces for each weekday. For example, if the first day of the week is Sunday, then W = 0, and a 1 is printed in the left corner of the screen. If it is a Monday, then W = 1, and the first "1" is printed 4 spaces over. Likewise, if the first weekday is Saturday, then W = 6, and the 1 is printed 24 spaces from the left. If you have a wider printer available, you can change the COL to a larger number.

Line 130 stops the program if the current date equals the maximum number of days in the month, DM. If they are not equal, the current date is incremented by 1 day in the next line. Line 150 checks whether the date was printed for Saturday. If W = 6, then the computer's printing position must be at the right-hand margin of the output. In that case, the weekday loop is exited, and W = 0 is set for Sunday. If it is not Saturday, line 160 increments the weekday. Once the weekday loop is exited, line 190 supplies a **PRINT** to stop printing on that line and start a new line. When this program is run for 31 days in the month and the first weekday = 1, the output is

SUN	MON	TUE	WED	THU	FRI	SAT
	1	2	3	4	5	6
7	8	9	10	11	12	13
14	15	16	17	18	19	20
21	22	23	24	25	26	27
28	29	30	31			

CHAPTER 12
Money Matters

If you ever bought something on credit, you probably were surprised—too late—at how much interest you had to pay. Even an apparently low interest rate of 10% can cost you a lot of money over 20 or 30 years. Your computer can help you shop around for the best rates available by calculating the interest charges. For example, which is better: a 14% loan for 25 years, or a 12% loan for 30 years?

Getting Your IRA Up

You can use your computer to estimate the amount you may have by investing in an Individual Retirement Account (IRA). IRAs allow working people to invest up to $2,000 a year in a tax-deferred account. No taxes are paid until you start collecting from the account, after age 59 1/2. However, IRA interest rates vary from one savings vehicle to another, and they may also depend on the current Money Market rates. Depending on performance, you may do better by investing in stocks that have shown good growth. Only you can decide what is best in your situation. However, your computer can help you make an investment decision by calculating how much may be available for different interest rates and time periods. The following program calculates the interest on a single principal deposit you might put into an IRA. This program is also useful for calculating interest on any deposit. For a regular bank savings account, however, you would need to subtract the federal income tax on the interest. The result depends on your tax bracket. In addition, Congress passed a law in 1982 to allow monthly federal withholding of taxes from interest payments. When all is considered, you can see that it is not easy to calculate years in advance how much you may accumulate. Nevertheless, look at the following program for an IRA.

```
  5 REM INTEREST ACCUMULATION BY LOOP
 10 PRINT "PRINCIPAL=?";
 20 INPUT P
 30 PRINT P
 40 PRINT "YEARS=?";
 50 INPUT Y
 60 PRINT Y
 70 PRINT "INTEREST RATE(PERCENT)=?";
 80 INPUT I
 90 PRINT I
100 LET I=I/100
110 SCROLL
120 PRINT "YEAR    PRINCIPAL   INTEREST"
130 FOR T=1 TO Y
140 LET IN=INT (100*P*I+.5)/100
150 LET P=P+IN
160 SCROLL
170 PRINT T;TAB 8;P;TAB 19;IN
180 NEXT T
```

Try running this program, in which PRINCIPAL=2000, YEARS=10, and INTEREST=12. You will observe the output scrolling up the screen as

YEAR	PRINCIPAL	INTEREST
1	2240	240
2	2508.8	268.8
3	2809.86	301.06
4	3147.04	337.18
5	3524.68	377.64
6	3947.64	422.96
7	4421.36	473.72
8	4951.92	530.56
9	5546.15	594.23
10	6211.69	665.54

The program displays the interest and your new principal every year. For example, after the first year, you made $240 in interest, which was added to your original principal to give your new principal of $2,240. After 10 years, you have more than tripled your investment of $2,000. Now try running the program for a 40-year period. You may want to use **FAST** mode for faster results. Note that you can press **BREAK** while the program is running, switch to **FAST**, and then press **CONT** to continue from where you stopped. If you have less than 2K of memory, such as in the standard Sinclair ZX-81, the display will stop scrolling on the 19th year, with a report code of 4. This happens because the display file that maintains the data for the screen, your program, and the space taken by BASIC for internal support has used up 1K. Notice that when the program was run for only 10 years, the report code did not appear, because the display file was not showing as much data on the screen. Just press **CONT** to continue.

If you had invested $2,000 at age 19, then you could start collecting from your IRA 40 years later, at age 59 1/2. Your original $2,000 may be worth $186,101.72, assuming that the interest rate remains constant at 12% over the 40-year period.

In the Interest Accumulation program, lines 10 through 90 prompt you to input the required data. Notice that there is no error checking in the program, so someone can enter a negative number and get an erroneous result. Line 100 converts to a decimal the interest, I, that is input as a percent. Lines 110 and 160 scroll the calculations up the screen.

Lines 130 through 180 make up a **FOR-NEXT** loop to do the interest calculations and print the results on the screen. Line 140 rounds off the interest, IN, to two decimal places after first calculating it as P*I. Notice that we round up to the next highest penny. Line 150 adds the interest to the principal, thereby yielding the new principal, and line 170 prints the results.

Did You Give at the Office?

You can make even more money off an IRA if you keep adding $2,000 every year. Many people just give at the office by contributing through their paychecks. Let's modify the Interest program so that $2,000 can be added each year. We'll assume that you put in $2,000 as one lump sum at the start of each year. After the new principal is printed by line 170, the following line 175 should be inserted in the program for adding $2,000 to the new principal in each pass through the loop.

        175 **LET** P = P + 2000

If you run this program in which years = 10, the accumulated principal will be $39,309.18 instead of the $6,211.69 that you got by investing only $2,000 once. For 40 years, you now get $1,718,285 instead of $186,101.72. Just as the IRA advertisements indicate, you can become a millionaire. Unfortunately, if inflation is 12% a year, you might be paying $2,000 for a sack of groceries by the time you become a millionaire. Your computer, however, does give you confidence in figuring the interest calculations, allowing you to shop around for the best investment instead of relying on ads.

Compounding Interest

Lenders like to proclaim that you get the maximum rate of return when your interest is compounded daily, instead of once a year. Although compound interest does pay you more, it also gives lenders a reason to collect compound interest *from you*, too, on loans they issue.

To compound the interest per day in your program, divide the interest per year by 365 days. (Let's assume that the loan doesn't need a leap year day.) To make the program able to calculate interest for any period, we'll let the user input the number of periods per year that interest is paid, by adding the following lines

```
92 PRINT "PERIODS PER YEAR=?";
94 INPUT PER
96 PRINT PER
```

Period designates how many times a year interest is paid or collected. For example, if the interest is paid monthly, then there are 12 periods per year. If the interest is paid daily, then there are 365 periods per year. Now change in line 100 the interest per year to decimal interest per period with

```
100 I=I/PER/100
```

Note that this expression is shorter than the alternate version of

```
100 I=I/(100*PER)
```

which requires a byte for the *, and 2 bytes for the left and right parentheses. The first version of line 100 uses 2 fewer bytes, because only a division sign, /, is needed. To compute interest, change line 150 back to

```
150 LET P=P+IN
```

as it was for the first program above for an IRA. In lines 120 and 130, use

```
120 PRINT "PERIOD   PRINCIPAL   INTEREST"
130 FOR T=1 TO PER*Y
```

to calculate the interest per period. This change is necessary now that the interest, I, is expressed per period. The term PER*Y indicates that the interest will be calculated from the first period to the total number of periods, PER*Y. In other words, if you are making monthly payments for 30 years, then

        PER=12

        PER*Y=12*30=360

and you will make 360 monthly payments. Run this compound interest program in which

        PRINCIPAL=2000

        YEARS=1

        INTEREST=12

        PERIODS=365

Notice that you begin by making 66 cents in interest per day until the 36th day, when the interest increases to 67 cents per day. If you don't want to watch the daily interest, either switch to **FAST** mode, or insert the line

        165 **IF** T<PER*Y **THEN GOTO** 180

Now nothing will be printed until this final entry:

        365   2254.96   0.74

When you compare this figure with the $2,240, computing the interest once a year, you will see that you will have made an extra $14.96 by the end of the year, if the interest is compounded daily. Now try the 40-year period with compound interest. Note that this time, you should use 365.25 periods per year to account for leap years. Even when run in **FAST** mode, the program takes about 7 minutes to do all the calculations, unless you add a line like

        165 **IF** T<PER*Y **THEN GOTO** 180

An efficient way of speeding things up is to eliminate unnecessary recalculations. For example, you can include the lines

        125 **LET** U=PER*Y

        165 **IF** T<U **THEN GOTO** 180

Now the PER*Y is not recalculated every time the loop occurs. Since this figure is a constant anyway, the computer does not have to recalculate it each time in the loop. The following program executes faster than the original version

        165 **IF** T<PER*Y **THEN GOTO** 180

When the calculations are done, you will see

        14610   242827.85   79.75

After 14,610 periods, your original investment of $2,000 has grown to $242,827.85 by daily compound interest, as compared to $186,101.72 by simple yearly interest. You certainly do make much more money with daily compound interest. Likewise, lenders get much more back when they loan money using compound interest. Property loans, however, are usually compounded once a month rather than once a day.

The Quick and Dirty Way

Although the interest results are accurate, the computer does take a long time to do the loop calculations if the interest is compounded every day. A faster, but slightly less accurate method, is to use a formula to compound interest.

In the case of 12% interest compounded only once a year, we have

        Initial Total Principal = 2000

        Total after 1st year = 2000*1.12 = 2240

        Total after 2nd year = 2240*1.12 = 2508.8

        Total after 3rd year = 2508.8*1.12 = 2809.86

These figures indicate that the total for any year equals 100% of the previous year's total. We can then write

        Total after 3rd year = 2000*1.12*1.12*1.12

                             = 2000*1.12**3

where the ** is the exponentiation operator found on key **H**. You will see a syntax error if you try to get a ** by pressing the * on the **B** key twice. You must use the **H** key. Try this program:

```
10 PRINT "EXPONENT";
20 INPUT E
30 PRINT 2000*1.12**E
40 GOTO 10
```

The output is shown below for different values of T.

T	Result
0	2000
1	2240
2	2508.8
3	2809.856
4	3147.0387
5	3524.6834
6	3947.6454
7	4421.3628
8	4951.9264
9	5546.1575
10	6211.6964
. .	
. .	
40	186101.94

You can see that these results are within a penny of those calculated by the loop method.

Now let's try the exponent method for compound interest. This program has the same input technique as our earlier examples.

```
5 REM INTEREST BY EXPONENTS
10 PRINT "PRINCIPAL=?";
20 INPUT P
30 PRINT P
40 PRINT "YEARS=?";
```

```
 50 INPUT Y
 60 PRINT Y
 70 PRINT "INTEREST RATE(PERCENT)=?";
 80 INPUT I
 90 PRINT I
100 PRINT "PERIODS PER YEAR=";
110 INPUT PER
120 PRINT PER
130 LET I=I/PER/100
140 FOR T=1 TO PER*Y
150 SCROLL
160 PRINT T;TAB 12;INT (100*P*(1+I)**T+.5)/100
170 NEXT T
```

When you run the program for Interest by Exponents, you will notice that the program runs even slower than the previous method of accumulating principal in a loop. The reason is that the computer takes much longer to calculate an exponent than a product. For example, try this test program in **FAST** mode, using a **RUN** 200 so that you don't delete the Interest program in memory.

```
200 FOR K=1 TO 1000
210 LET X=K**2
220 NEXT K
230 PRINT "DONE"
```

Notice that the program takes about 2 minutes to complete. If you replace line 210 with

```
210 LET X=K*2
```

it will take only about 9 seconds. Once you have seen the difference in times, delete lines 200 through 230.

The exponent formula is fine for quickly calculating a specific period, but slow for use in generating tables. Since in many cases we just want to know the total principal, make the following changes to your program to calculate only the final principal.

```
140 LET T=PER*Y
150 PRINT "PERIODS   FINAL PRINCIPAL"
160 PRINT T;TAB 12;INT (100*P*(1+I)**T+.5)/100,,,
170 GOTO 10
```

Line 140 sets T to the maximum number of periods, which is the periods per year multiplied by the number of years. Line 150 prints a title. The only change to line 160 is the addition of three commas at the end of the line. This addition prints a blank line before the new principal prompt. An alternative would have been

```
170 PRINT
180 GOTO 10
```

but by adding the three commas, we've saved several bytes of memory. Line 170, **GOTO** 10, is introduced for convenience in adding more input.

A sample run of the program with these changes is

```
PRINCIPAL=?2000
YEARS=?40
INTEREST RATE(PERCENT)=?12
PERIODS PER YEAR=?365.25
PERIODS   FINAL PRINCIPAL
14610      242829.7
```

Notice that the final principal here is \$242,829.7 instead of the \$242,827.85 calculated by the loop technique. The exponent method is not as accurate as the loop method because the former uses logarithms, and only a certain precision is maintained in the computer. The loop method is correct to the penny every time. However, the exponent method is definitely much faster if you just want the approximate final value.

Monthly Payments

Generally, property loans are paid back in equal payments every month. The formula to calculate the monthly payment is derived from the amount borrowed, the interest rate, and the number of months desired to pay back the loan, as in

$$P = \frac{A*I*(1+I)**N}{(1+I)**N-1}$$

where

P is the monthly payment

A is the original amount borrowed

I is the decimal interest per month

N is the total number of months needed to repay the loan

P is also called the periodic payment, because the payment is made regularly or periodically. On a monthly basis, the number of periods is 12; on a quarterly basis, 4.

As with the compound interest programs, you get I by dividing the interest per year by the periods per year. If the interest rate per year is 11%, then I=.11/12 is the monthly interest rate.
For example, a $50,000 loan at 11% interest for 25 years (25X12=300 periods) gives

$$P = \frac{50000*.11/12(1+.11/12)**300}{(1+.11/12)**300-1}$$

P=$490.06 per month as the payment.

You can print the result using the formula alone, but it is often more convenient to use a program, as shown below. When you enter and run this program, change the period to 365, 365.25 (leap-year inclusion), then to 52, and finally to 4 to see the effect on the payments.

```
5 REM PERIODIC PAYMENTS BY EXPONENTS
10 PRINT "AMOUNT=?";
```

```
20 INPUT A
30 PRINT A
40 PRINT "YEARS=?";
50 INPUT Y
60 PRINT Y
70 PRINT "INTEREST RATE(PERCENT)=?";
80 INPUT I
90 PRINT I
100 PRINT "PERIODS PER YEAR=?";
110 INPUT PER
120 PRINT PER
130 LET I=I/PER/100
140 LET N=PER*Y
150 LET P=A*I*(1+I)**N/((1+I)**N-1)
160 PRINT "PAYMENT PER PERIOD=";INT
(100*P+.5)/100,,,
170 GOTO 10
```

In addition to calculating the monthly payments, let's also find out how much the loan is really going to cost you. To determine the total amount you will pay, TOT, multiply the monthly payments by the number of payments.

$$TOT = P*N$$

The interest charges, IN, will be the total you've paid, minus the amount borrowed, A, as in

$$IN = TOT-A$$

You can easily include these adjustments to the program for Periodic Payments.

```
152 LET TOT=P*N
154 LET IN=TOT-A
156 PRINT "TOTAL COST=";INT (100*TOT+.5)/1 00
```

158 **PRINT** "TOTAL INTEREST = ";**INT** (100*IN + .5)/100

Now run this program for a $50,000 loan at 14%, with monthly payments for 25 years. You will see

```
AMOUNT = ?50000
YEARS = ?25
INTEREST RATE(PERCENT) = ?14
PERIODS PER YEAR = ?12
TOTAL COST = 180564.16
TOTAL INTEREST = 130564.16
PAYMENT PER PERIOD = 601.88
```

Your $50,000 loan would cost you $130,564.16 in interest over the 25-year period. Suppose you could get the same loan at 12% for 30 years. This looks like a bargain, since you would pay 2% less in interest, and the monthly payments would be smaller. Let's examine this "bargain" with your computer.

```
AMOUNT = ?50000
YEARS = ?30
INTEREST = ?12
PERIODS PER YEAR = ?12
TOTAL COST = 185150.27
TOTAL INTEREST = 135150.27
PAYMENT PER PERIOD = 514.31
```

The 12% loan actually costs you $135,150 in interest, compared to the $130,564 interest cost of the 14% loan. It is true that the monthly payments are smaller for the 12% loan, but only because you're making payments for a longer time.

As another example, how much does a car loan of $5,000 at 14% over 3 years cost?

```
AMOUNT = ?5000
YEARS = ?3
INTEREST = ?14
PERIODS PER YEAR = ?12
TOTAL COST = 6151.97
TOTAL INTEREST = 1151.97
PAYMENT PER PERIOD = 170.89
```

If you can get the same loan at 12%, you will see

```
AMOUNT=?5000
YEARS=?3
INTEREST=?12
PERIODS PER YEAR=?12
TOTAL COST=5978.58
TOTAL INTEREST=978.58
PAYMENT PER PERIOD=166.07
```

In this case you would save about $173 with the 12% loan.

Bankers' Way

If you want to check loan statements from a bank or some other lender, you must do it the bankers' way.

Although the monthly payment we calculated in the last section is correct, there may be a slight error of a penny in a month's calculation because of the rounding off of numbers. For example, run the Periodic Payment program for a $50,000 loan, over 25 years, at 11% with monthly payments. You will get the following results:

```
TOTAL COST=147016.96
TOTAL INTEREST=97016.96
PAYMENT PER PERIOD=490.06
```

Now **STOP** the program and **PRINT** P. You will see

```
490.05654
```

This is the figure that was rounded off to $490.06.

Every month, the portions applied to pay off the original amount, the principal, and the interest are also rounded off. In any month, you may have too much or too little applied to the principal or the interest. The actual amounts will depend on the rounding off of the monthly payment. To duplicate the bank's method, calculate all payments toward interest and the amount borrowed every month. Then round off calculations to two decimal places, just as the bank does on your loan statement.

The following program calculates monthly payments and the amounts applied toward the interest and toward paying off the loan. The program can print out a table showing the period, the principal built up to pay off the loan, and the total interest paid so far. At the end, the computer will output the total amount you've paid and the total interest charges. If you don't want the table, only the final figures can be shown.

```
5 REM EXACT INTEREST
10 PRINT "AMOUNT=";
20 INPUT A
30 PRINT A
40 PRINT "YEARS=";
50 INPUT Y
60 PRINT Y
70 PRINT "INTEREST RATE(PERCENT)=";
80 INPUT I
90 PRINT I
100 PRINT "PERIODS/YEAR=";
110 INPUT PER
120 PRINT PER
130 PRINT "TABLE?YES OR NO-";
140 INPUT T$
150 PRINT T$
160 LET H=100
170 LET I=I/PER/H
180 LET N=PER*Y
190 LET P=A*I*(1+I)**N/((1+I)**N-1)
200 LET P=INT (H*P+.5)/H
210 LET PAY=P
220 LET PRI=0
230 LET IN=0
240 SCROLL
```

```
250 IF T$="NO" THEN GOTO 270
260 PRINT "PER PRINCIPAL INTEREST   BALANCE"
270 FOR J=1 TO N
280 IF J=N THEN LET PAY=INT (H*A*(1+I)+.5)/H
290 LET MIC=INT (H*A*I+.5)/H
300 LET PRI=INT (H*(PRI+PAY-MIC)+.5)/H
310 LET IN=INT (H*(IN+MIC)+.5)/H
320 LET A=INT (H*(A+MIC-PAY)+.5)/H
330 IF T$="NO" THEN GOTO 360
340 SCROLL
350 PRINT J;TAB 4;PRI;TAB 14;IN;TAB 24;A
360 NEXT J
370 SCROLL
380 PRINT "PAYMENT PER PERIOD=";P
390 SCROLL
400 PRINT "FINAL PAYMENT=";PAY
410 IF T$="YES" THEN STOP
420 SCROLL
430 PRINT "PER PRINCIPAL INTEREST   BALANCE"
440 SCROLL
450 PRINT J-1;TAB 4;PRI;TAB 14;IN;TAB 24;A
```

Lines 10 through 150 prompt you for the information that the program requires. Line 160 stores the constant 100 in the variable H. This variable is used 13 times in place of 100. If you try using a 100 instead of H, then the program will stop while doing a table for some combination of inputs, with a report code of 4. This report code indicates an out-of-memory condition, because the program, the variables, and the display file exceed the standard 2K bytes in your T/S 1000 computer. If you have additional memory, such as the 16K RAM Module, you won't run out of memory so easily. In fact, minimizing memory size is why the question marks were left out of the prompts in lines 10, 40, 70, and 100 to save 4 bytes. For further reductions, the **REM** statement of line 5 could be cut. However, it is a good idea to leave some internal documentation in the program.

Line 170 computes the decimal interest per period. In line 180, a variable, N, is defined for convenience and memory efficiency. N is set to the total number of periods required to pay off the loan. Line 190 computes the payment, P, per monthly period, and line 200 rounds it off to the nearest cent. Line 210 defines a new variable, PAY, as the initial value of the payment. This variable represents the amount you pay every month until the final month, when PAY will be set equal to the amount remaining, as shown in line 280. This guarantees that the loan will be paid off in the final month, no matter what errors have accumulated from rounding off. In practice, the final payment will be off by a small percentage.

Line 220 defines the initial amount of the monthly payment applied toward the principal, equal to 0, PRI=0. The principal, PRI, will then build up, month by month, until it equals the amount borrowed, and the loan is then paid off. Line 230 sets the initial amount of the interest charges, IN=0. Line 240 is a **SCROLL** to allow continuous printing of output. Since you want a long table, it is best to **SCROLL** so that the computer won't stop the program when the screen gets full. Notice that a **SCROLL** must be put before every **PRINT** statement from now on. Otherwise, you will see an error when the computer tries to print something below the 22nd line of the screen.

Line 250 avoids printing the table header if you don't want a table. Line 260 prints the headers for the table calculations: PER for period number, PRINGIPAL for the principal accumulated to pay off the loan, INTEREST for the total interest you've paid so far, and BALANCE for the balance.

Lines 270 through 360 form the loop to do the monthly calculations. First, the interest charges for the month are calculated as

$$\text{Monthly Interest Charge} = \text{Amount} * \text{Monthly Interest Rate}$$
$$= A * I$$

This rate is rounded off to the cent and stored in the variable, MIC (Monthly Interest Charge). Ideally, it would be better to use longer names, such as MONTHLY INTEREST CHARGE, instead of MIC. However, with only 2K bytes, you must be conservative in using long variable names, since each extra letter requires a byte of memory. Using a 5-letter variable name 10 times in your program would need 40 bytes more than a one-letter name used 10 times— and take longer to execute. On the other hand, short names do make it harder for a user to understand a program listing.

Line 300 calculates the portion of your payment that is applied toward the principal. The amount applied to principal equals the monthly payment minus the monthly interest charge(=PAY-MIC).

Now let's add this figure to the previous principal to find the total amount that has been applied to paying off the loan.

    PRI+PAY-MIC

represents the total amount applied so far to paying off the principal, or amount borrowed. This amount is rounded off to the nearest cent and stored as the new total Principal, PRI.

Line 310 adds the accumulated total interest, IN, to the latest Monthly Interest Charge, MIC,

    IN+MIC

and rounds off the result to the nearest cent. This result is stored as the new total interest charge, IN, paid.

Line 320 computes the amount you have left to pay. In any month, you still owe

    Amount Owed+Monthly Interest Charge-Monthly Payment

or

    A+MIC-PAY

This amount, then, is rounded off to the nearest cent and stored as the new amount that you owe.

If T$ = NO, then line 330 skips over lines 340 and 350, which prints the table data of

>   J-period
>
>   PRI-total principal paid toward the amount borrowed
>
>   IN-total interest charges paid
>
>   A-amount remaining to be paid

Line 380 prints the payment per period, P, and line 400 prints the final payment. You will see from the following examples that the final payment does not usually equal the payment per period.

Line 410 stops the program if the user has requested a table. Without a table, the final results of the loop are printed as a check to show that all calculations were performed. Note that you had to use J-1 instead of J because after the loop, J = N + 1.

This program can be used to print tables of loan amounts up to $99,999. Above this amount, you run into the problem of having only 32 characters displayed on a line. For higher values, you will have to print the amount remaining on a second line. For example,

```
260 PRINT "PER PRINCIPAL    INTEREST"
262 SCROLL
264 PRINT TAB 8;"BALANCE"
350 PRINT J;TAB 4;PRI;TAB 16;IN
352 SCROLL
354 PRINT TAB 8;A
```

Notice that more spacing between numbers is allowed in line 350. This change also reduces the display file size, so you won't be so cramped for memory. However, the computer does take longer to print a table.

Now run the original program (without lines 260 to 354 above) for a $50,000 loan for 25 years, at 11% interest, with monthly payments, and enter YES in answer to the TABLE question. You will see

```
AMOUNT=50000

YEARS=25

INTEREST RATE(PERCENT)=11

PERIODS PER YEAR=12

TABLE?YES OR NO-YES
```

In **SLOW** mode, you will see these results come scrolling up the screen:

PER	PRINCIPAL	INTEREST	BALANCE
1	31.73	458.33	49968.27
2	63.75	916.37	49936.25
3	96.06	1374.12	49903.94

If you get tired of watching these numbers appear on the screen, then press the **SPACE** key to **BREAK**. You may have to press it several times to get the computer's attention. Switch to **FAST** and press **CONT** to continue execution in **FAST** mode.

Even in **FAST** mode, the program takes several minutes to finish its calculations. Although you may think this method is slow, think how long it takes to get all these same calculations from the lender!

Finally, the computer will stop, and you will see the last screenful of output.

```
282 41907.15  96289.77  8092.85
283 42323.03  96363.95  7676.97

. . . . . . . . . . . . . . . .
294 49520.06  97007.88  479.94
300 50000     97012.28  0
PAYMENT PER PERIOD=490.06
FINAL PAYMENT=484.34
TOTAL PAID=147012.28
```

You made 300 payments to pay back the $50,000 loan. The lender got $97,012.28 in interest. You made 299 monthly payments of $490.06 and a final payment of $484.34 to account for the rounding off of errors in the monthly payment, principal, and interest.

If you just want the final figures, switch to **FAST** mode and run the program again. Now, when the TABLE question is asked, enter NO. You will get the answer in about 25 seconds, because the computer can skip all the **PRINT** statements in the table. You will see that all 300 payments were made, since PER = 300.

```
PAYMENT PER PERIOD = 490.06
FINAL PAYMENT = 484.34
TOTAL PAID = 147012.28
PER  PRINCIPAL  INTEREST  BALANCE
300  50000      97012.28  0
```

When you run the monthly 14% loan on $50,000 for 25 years, you will get

```
PAYMENT PER PERIOD = 601.88
FINAL PAYMENT = 603.15
TOTAL PAID = 180565.27
PER  PRINCIPAL  INTEREST  BALANCE
300  50000      130565.27  0
```

Now compare these figures to the approximate results from the program on Periodic Payments by Exponents that you ran earlier.

```
TOTAL COST = 180564.16
TOTAL INTEREST = 130564.16
PAYMENT PER PERIOD = 601.88
```

You can see that the payment per month in the Exact program is the same until the final payment, when it increases from $601.88 to $603.15. This increase occurs because the monthly payment was actually $601.88052. Since .88052 was not enough to get rounded up a penny, to $601.89, you actually pay a little less per month than you should. In the last month, your final payment is increased to make up for this discrepancy.

EPILOGUE
Looking Back/Looking Ahead

At this point, you've come a long way in learning about computers. Thinking back, you're probably amazed at how much you've learned in such a short time. By now, you've learned how to

- use your computer as a supercalculator
- write programs
- save and load programs from tape

But what's really important is that you've learned that computers are not mysterious oracles of wisdom which always give the right answer. Computers are a tool of the mind, and you have learned the basic skills of controlling this great tool.

By working with computers, you have also seen the importance of logical, clear thinking. Your computer does exactly what it's told—

no more, no less. You must tell the computer what to do and how to do it. You are in control.

In the second volume, you'll continue to learn about programming. You'll enhance your programming skills by learning about the advanced commands of BASIC. In the second book, you'll learn how to use these to

- deal efficiently with large amounts of data
- study a program for checkbook balancing and check data storage using your computer
- organize and retrieve easily an alphabetical list of items
- write video game programs
- bypass the normal restrictions of BASIC
- learn many more applications

The important thing to keep in mind is that programming is a skill. Like any other skill, you've got to keep practicing it to maintain it. Look around at your business and personal lives for opportunities to write programs. The more programs you write, the easier it will become. You may also wish to join or form a computer club. It's fun and interesting to meet other people with similar interests.

APPENDIX A
Magazine Articles of Interest
to T/S 1000 Users

Sync Magazine

GAMES AND PROGRAMS

Lunar Lander . . . . Jan./Feb. 1982—Vol. 2, No. 1
Battleship Solitaire . . . . Jan./Feb. 1982—Vol. 2, No. 1
Tioga Toads . . . . Jan./Feb. 1982—Vol. 2, No. 1
Dice and Train . . . . Jan./Feb. 1982—Vol. 2, No. 1
6 Shooter . . . . Mar./Apr. 1982—Vol. 2, No. 2
Isolation . . . . Mar./Apr. 1982—Vol. 2, No. 2
Space Warp . . . . May/June 1982—Vol. 2, No. 3
ZX Destroyer . . . . July/Aug. 1982—Vol. 2, No. 4
Galaxy Invaders . . . . July/Aug. 1982—Vol. 2, No. 4
Micro Invaders . . . . July/Aug. 1982—Vol. 2, No. 4
Comet Crusher . . . . July/Aug. 1982—Vol. 2, No. 4
Crossing the Astroid Belt . . . . July/Aug. 1982—Vol. 2, No. 4
Alien Treasure . . . . July/Aug. 1982—Vol. 2, No. 4

MATH

Understanding Floating-Point Arithmetic
Part One—Decimal and binary formats . . . . . . Jan./Feb. 1982—Vol. 2, No. 1
Linear Regression . . . . Jan./Feb. 1982—Vol. 2, No. 1
Understanding Floating-Point Arithmetic

SYNTAX Magazine

HARDWARE PROJECTS

TIPS AND HINTS

MACHINE LANGUAGE

BEGINNERS

APPENDIX B
Order of Priority of Operators

Operator	Priority
Slicing and Subscripting	12
All Functions	11
**	10
- (Unary Minus)	9
*,/	8
+,- (Binary Minus)	6
=,<=,>=,<,>,<>	5
NOT	4
AND	3
OR	2

Note: Operators of the same priority are evaluated left to right.

Report Codes

This table gives each report code, with a general description and a list of the statements and functions in which it can occur. In Chapter 21, under each statement or function, you will find a more detailed description of what the error reports mean.

Code	Meaning	Situations
Ø	Successful completion, or jump to line number bigger than any existing. A report with code Ø does not change the line number used by **CONT**.	Any
1	The control variable does not exist (has not been set up by a **FOR** statement), but there is an ordinary variable with the same name.	**NEXT**
2	An undefined variable has been used.	Any
	For a simple variable this will happen if the variable is used before it has been assigned to in a **LET** statement.	
	For a subscripted variable it will happen if the variable is used before it has been dimensioned in a **DIM** statement.	
	For a control variable in a **FOR** statement and if there is no ordinary simple variable with the same name.	
3	Subscript out of range. If the subscript is out of range (negative, or bigger than 65535), error B will result.	Subscripted variables
4	Not enough room in memory. Note that the line number in the report (after the /) may not be complete on the screen,	**LET, INPUT, DIM, PRINT, LIST, PLOT, UNPLOT, FOR,**

Report Codes

Code	Meaning	Situations
	because of the shortage of memory: for instance, 4/2Ø may appear as 4/2. See Chapter 9.	**GOSUB**. Sometimes during function evaluation.
5	No more room on the screen. **CONT** will make room by clearing the screen.	**PRINT, LIST, PLOT, UNPLOT**
6	Arithmetic overflow: calculations have led to a number greater than about 10^{38}.	Any arithmetic
7	No corresponding **GOSUB** for a **RETURN** statement.	**RETURN**
8	You have attempted an **INPUT** command (not allowed).	**INPUT**
9	**STOP** statement executed. **CONT** will not try to reexecute the **STOP** statement.	**STOP**
A	Invalid argument to certain functions.	**SQR, LN, ASN, ACS**
B	Integer out of range. When an integer is required, the floating-point argument is rounded to the nearest integer. If this is outside a suitable range, error B results.	**RUN, RAND, POKE, DIM, GOTO, GOSUB, LIST, PAUSE, PLOT, UNPLOT, CHR$, PEEK, USR**
	For array access, see also Report 3.	Array access
C	The text of the (string) argument of **VAL** does not form a valid numerical expression.	**VAL**
D	(i) Program interrupted by **BREAK**.	At the end of any statement, or in **LOAD, SAVE, LPRINT, LLIST,** or **COPY**.
	(ii) The **INPUT** line starts with **STOP**.	**INPUT**
E	Not used	
F	The program name provided is the empty string.	**SAVE**

APPENDIX D

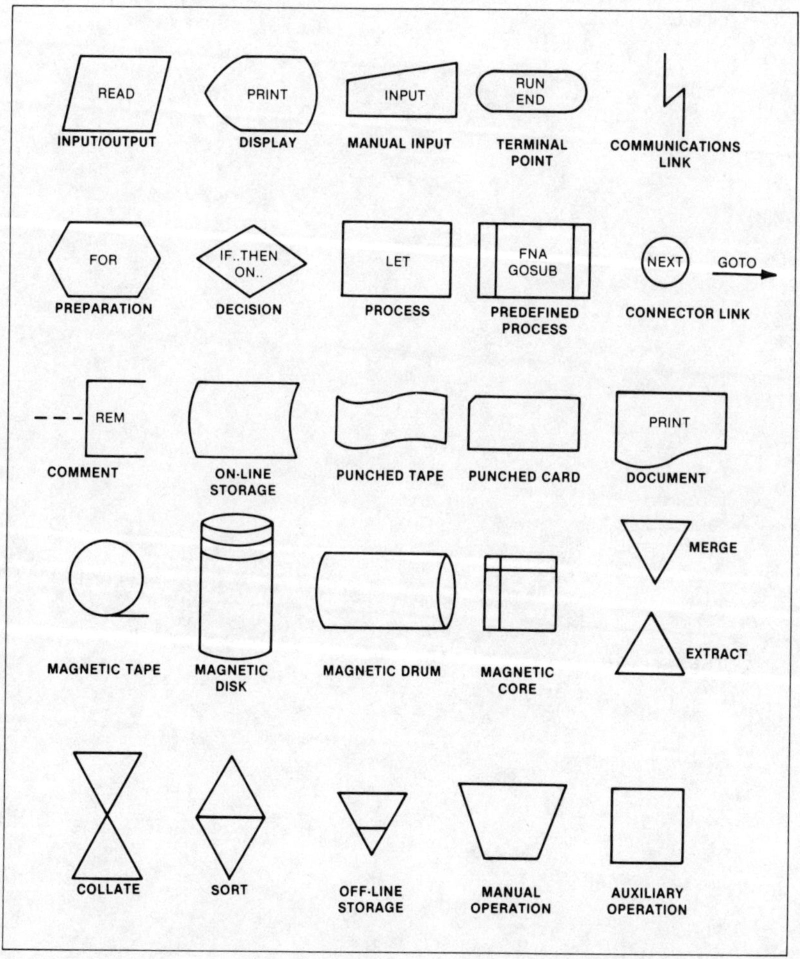

The ANSI Flow Chart Symbols

APPENDIX E
Derivation of the Periodic Payment Formula

Generally, the payment of a loan in equal installments includes portions towards both the interest and the principal.

the first month,

$$P = A*I + T1$$

in which

P = periodic payment

A = amount borrowed

I = decimal interest per period

For example, if the yearly interest is 12%, and the loan is paid monthly, then

$$I = \frac{12}{100*12} = .01$$

T1 = portion of payment that applies toward reducing the amount borrowed in the first month.

A*I = is the portion of the payment that applies toward the interest.

In the second month,

$$P=(A-T1)*I+T2$$

in which the amount owed is reduced by P1, the portion of the first payment that applied toward the amount borrowed in the first month.

Equations I and 2 can be set equal to one another, since they both have the same payment, P, as in

$$A*I+T1=(A-T1)*I+T2$$
$$=A*I\text{-}T1*I+T2$$

To solve for T2 in terms of T1, use

$$T2=T1*(1+I)$$

In the third month,

$$P=(A-T1-T2)*I+T3$$

Setting equation 2 equal to equation 3, and multiplying through by I, gives

$$A*I\text{-}T1*I+T2=A*I\text{-}T1*I\text{-}T2*I+T3$$

then

$$T2=\text{-}T2*I+T3$$

and so

$$T3=T2*(1+I)=T1*(1+I)**2$$

Now we can deduce that the last payment applying toward the amount borrowed can be expressed as

$$TN = T1*(1+I)**(N-1)$$

in which N is the total number of payments. Also, the last payment is

$$P = (A-T1-T2-T3...-(TN-1))*I+TN$$
$$P = TN*I+TN = TN*(1+I)$$

since we must pay off the loan by TN in the last payment. So

$$P = (T1*(1+I)**N-1)*(1+I)$$
$$P = T1*(1+I)**N$$
$$P = (P-A*I)*(1+I)**N$$

Solving this last equation for P gives

$$P = \frac{A*I*(1+I)**N}{(1+I)**N-1}$$

APPENDIX F
BASIC Symbols and Keys

Symbol	Key	Position
ABS	G	Below key
AND	2	Above key
ARCCOS	S	Below key
ARCSIN	A	Below key
ARCTAN	D	Below key
BREAK	SPACE	Above key
CHR$	U	Below key
CLEAR	X	Above key
CLS	V	Above key
CODE	I	Below key
CONT	C	Above key
COPY	Z	Above key
COS	W	Below key
DELETE	Ø	Above key
DIM	D	Above key
EDIT	1	On key
EXP	X	Below key
FAST	F	On key
FOR	F	Above key
FUNCTION	ENTER	On key

GOSUB	H	Above key
GOTO	G	Above key
IF	U	Above key
INKEY$	B	Below key
INPUT	I	Above key
INT	R	Below key
LEN	K	Below key
LET	L	Above key
LIST	K	Above key
LLIST	G	On key
LN	Z	Below key
LOAD	J	Above key
LPRINT	S	On key
NEW	A	Above key
NEXT	N	Above key
NOT	N	Below key
OR	W	On key
PAUSE	M	Above key
PEEK	O	Below key
PI	M	Below key
PLOT	Q	Above key
POKE	O	Above key
PRINT	P	Above key
RAND	T	Above key
REM	E	Above key
RETURN	Y	Above key
RND	T	Below key
RUN	R	Above key
SAVE	S	Above key
SGN	F	Below key
SIN	Q	Below key
SLOW	D	On key
SQR	H	Below key
STEP	E	On key
STOP	A	On key
STR$	Y	Below key
TAB	P	Below key
TAN	E	Below key
THEN	3	On key

TO	4	On key
UNPLOT	W	Above key
USR	L	Below key
VAL	J	Below key

Reprinted from Timex *User Manual* by permission of Timex Computer Corporation

Function	Type of operand	Result
	(x)	
ABS	number	Absolute magnitude.
ACS	number	Arccosine in radians. Error A if x not in the range -1 to $+1$.
AND	binary operation, right operand always a number.	
	Numeric left operand:	$\text{A } \textbf{AND } \text{B} = \begin{cases} \text{A if B} \neq 0 \\ 0 \text{ if B} = 0 \end{cases}$
	String left operand:	$\text{A\$ } \textbf{AND } \text{B} = \begin{cases} \text{A\$ if B} \neq 0 \\ \text{"" if B} = 0 \end{cases}$
ASN	number	Arcsine in radians. Error A if x not in the range -1 to $+1$.

ATN	number	Arctangent in radians.
CHR$	number	The character whose code is x, rounded down to the nearest integer. Error B if x not in the range Ø to 255.
CODE	string	The code of the first character in x (or Ø if x is empty string).
COS	number (in radians)	Cosine
EXP	number	e^x.
INKEY$	none	Reads the keyboard. The result is the character representing (in ▉ mode) the key pressed if there is exactly one, else the empty string.
INT	number	Integer part (always rounds down).
LEN	string	Length.
LN	number	Natural logarithm (to base e). Error A if $x <= Ø$.
NOT	number	Ø if $x \neq Ø$, 1 if $x = Ø$. **NOT** has priority 4.
OR	binary operation, both operands numbers	A **OR** B = $\begin{cases} 1 \text{ if } B \neq Ø. \\ A \text{ if } B = Ø. \end{cases}$ **OR** has priority 2.
PEEK	number	The value of the byte in memory whose address is x (rounded to the nearest integer). Error B if x not in the range Ø to 65535.
PI	none	π (3.14159265...)
RND	none	The next pseudo-random number y in a sequence generated by taking the powers of 75 modulo 65537, subtracting 1 and dividing by 65536. $Ø <= y < 1$.
SGN	number	Signum: the sign $(-1, Ø$ or $+1)$ of x.

SIN	number (in radians)	Sine.
SQR	number	Square root. Error B if x < $\emptyset$.
STR$	number	The string of characters that would be displayed if x were printed.
TAN	number (in radians)	Tangent.
USR	number	Calls the machine code subroutine whose starting address is x. On return, the result is the contents of the bc register pair.
VAL	string	Evaluates x (without its bounding quotes) as a numerical expression. Error C if x contains a syntax error, or gives a string value. Other errors possible, depending on the expression.
–	number	Negation

The following are binary operations:

+	Addition (on numbers), or concatenation (on strings)
–	Subtraction
*	Multiplication
/	Division
**	Raising to a power. Error B if left operand is negative.
=	Equals
>	Greater than
<	Less than
< =	Less than or equal to
> =	Greater than or equal to
< >	Not equal to

Both operands must be of the same type. The result is a number, 1 if the comparison holds, and $\emptyset$ if it does not.

Statements

In this list,

@	represents a single letter
v	represents a variable
x,y,z	represents numerical expressions
m,n	represents numerical expressions that are rounded to the nearest integer

e   represents an expression
f   represents a string-valued expression
s   represents a statement

Note that arbitrary expressions are allowed everywhere (except for the line number at the beginning of a statement).

All statements except **INPUT** can be used either as commands or in programs (although they may be more sensible in one than the other).

CLEAR

Deletes all variables, freeing the space they occupied.

CLS

(CLear Screen) Clears the display file. See Chapter 26 concerning the display file.

CONT

Suppose a/b were the last report with a non-zero. Then **CONT** has the effect
$$\textbf{GOTO } b \text{ if } a \neq 9$$
$$\textbf{GOTO } b+1 \text{ if } a = 9 \text{ (}\textbf{STOP}$$
statement)

COPY

Sends a copy of the display to the printer, if attached; otherwise does nothing.
Report D if **BREAK** pressed.

DIM @ $(n_1,...,n_k)$

Deletes any array with the name @ and sets up an array of numbers with k dimensions $n_1,...,n_k$. Initializes all the values to 0.
Error 4 occurs if there is no room to fit the array in. An array is undefined until it is dimensioned in a **DIM** statement.

DIM @ $\$(n_1, ..., n_k)$

Deletes any array or string with the name @ $ and sets up an array of characters with k dimensions $n_1, ..., n_k$. Initializes all the values to $''''$. This can be considered as an array of strings of fixed length n_k, with $k-1$ dimensions $n_1, ..., n_{k-1}$.
Error 4 occurs if there is no room to fit the array in. An array is undefined until it is dimensioned in a **DIM** statement.

FAST

Starts fast mode, in which the display file is displayed only at the end of the program, while **INPUT** data is being typed in, or during a pause.

FOR @ =x **TO** y   **FOR** @ =x **TO** y **STEP** 1

FOR @ =x **TO** y **STEP** z

Deletes any simple variable and sets up a control variable with value x, limit y, step z, and looping address 1 more than the line number of the **FOR** statement (−1 if it is a command). Checks if the initial value is greater (if step $> = \emptyset$) or less (if step $< \emptyset$) than the limit, and if so, then skips to statement **NEXT** @ at the beginning of a line. See **NEXT** @ .
Error 4 occurs if there is no room for the control variable.

GOSUB n

Pushes the number of the **GOSUB** statement onto a stack; then as **GOTO** n.
Error 4 can occur if there are not enough **RETURN**s.

GOTO n

Jumps to line n (or, if there is none, to the first line after that).

IF x **THEN** s

If x is true (non-zero), then s is executed.
The form '**IF** x **THEN** line number' is not allowed.

INPUT v

Stops (with no special prompt) and waits for the user to type in an expression; the value of this is assigned to v. In fast mode, the display file is displayed. **INPUT** cannot be used as a command; error 8 occurs if you try.
If the first character in the **INPUT** line is **STOP**, the program stops with report D.

LET v=e

Assigns the value of e to the variable v.
LET cannot be omitted.
A simple variable is undefined until it is assigned to in a **LET** or **INPUT** statement.
If v is a subscripted string variable, or a sliced string variable (substring), then the assignment is *Procrustean*: the string value of e is either truncated or filled out with spaces to the right, to make it the same length as the variable v.

LIST   **LIST** Ø

LIST n

Lists the program on the TV screen, starting at line n, and makes n the current line.
Error 4 or 5 if the listing is too long to fit on the screen; **CONT** will do exactly the same again.

LLIST

LLIST n

LLIST 0

Like **LIST**, but using the printer instead of the television.
Should do nothing if the printer is not attached.
Stops with Report D if **BREAK** is pressed.

LOAD f

Looks for a program called f on tape and loads it and its variables. If f = '''', then loads the first program available.
If **BREAK** is pressed, then
   (i) if no program has yet been read in from tape, stops with report D and old program;
   (ii) if part of a program has been read in, then executes **NEW**.

LPRINT ...

Like **PRINT**, but using the printer instead of the television. A line of text is sent to the printer
   (i) when printing spills over from one line to the next,
   (ii) after an **LPRINT** statement that does not end in a comma or a semicolon,

   (iii) when a comma or **TAB** item requires a new line, or
   (iv) at the end of the program, if there is anything left unprinted.
In an **AT** item, only the column number has any affect; the line number is ignored. An **AT** item never sends a line of text to the printer.
There should be no effect if the printer is absent.
Stops with report D if **BREAK** is pressed.

NEW

Restarts the BASIC system, deleting program and variables and using the memory up to but not including the byte whose address is in the system variable RAMTOP (bytes 16388 and 16389).

NEXT @

   (i) Finds the control variable @.
   (ii) Adds its step to its value.
   (iii) If the step $> = 0$ and the value $>$ the limit; or if the step < 0 and the value $<$ the limit, then jumps to the looping line.
Error 1 if there is no control variable @.

PAUSE n

Stops computing and displays the display file for n frames (at 5Ø frames per second) or until a key is pressed. Ø <= n <= 65535, else error B. If n >= 32767, then the pause is not timed, but lasts until a key is pressed.

PLOT m,n

Blacks in the pixel (|m|,|n|); moves the **PRINT** position to just after that pixel.
Ø <= |m| <= 63, Ø <= |n| <= 43, else error B.

POKE m,n

Writes the value n to the byte in store with address m.
Ø <= m <= 65535, −255 <= n <= 255, else error B.

PRINT ...

The '...' is a sequence of **PRINT** items, separated by commas or semicolons. They are written to the display file for display on the television. The position (line and column) where the next character is to be printed is called the **PRINT** position.
A **PRINT** item can be
  (i)   empty, i.e., nothing
  (ii) a numerical expression

First, a minus sign is printed if the value is negative.
Now let x be the modulus of the value.
If $x <= 10^{-5}$ or $x >= 10^{13}$, then it is printed using scientific notation. The mantissa part has up to eight digits (with no trailing zeros), and the decimal point (absent if only one digit) is after the first. The exponent part is E, followed by + or −, followed by one or two digits.
Otherwise x is printed in ordinary decimal notation with up to eight significant digits, and no trailing zeros after the decimal point. A decimal point right at the beginning is always followed by a zero, so, for instance, .Ø3 and Ø.3 are printed as such.
Ø is printed as a single digit Ø.

  (iii) a string expression.
The tokens in the string are expanded, possibly with a space before or after.

The quote image character prints as ''.
Unused characters and control characters
print as ?.
(iv) **AT** m,n
The **PRINT** position is changed to line m
(counting from the top), column n (counting
from the left). $0 <= |m| <= 21$, $0 <= |n| <= 31$, else error B. If $|m| = 22$ or 23, error 5.
(v) **TAB** n
n is reduced modulo 32. Then, the **PRINT**
position is moved to column n, staying on the
same line unless this would involve backspac-
ing, in which case it moves on to the next line.
$0 <= n <= 255$, else error B.

A semicolon between two items leaves the
PRINT position unchanged, so that the second item follows immediately after the first. A
comma, on the other hand, moves the **PRINT**
position on at least one place; and after that,
as many as are necessary to leave it in column
0 or 16, moving to a new line if necessary.
At the end of the **PRINT** statement, if it
does not end in a semicolon or comma, a new
line is started.

Error 4 (out of memory) can occur with 3K or
less of memory.
Error 5 means that the screen is filled.

In both cases, the cure is **CONT**, which will
clear the screen and allow the program
to continue.

RAND   **RAND** 0

RAND n   Sets the system variable (called SEED) used to
generate the next value of **RND**. If $n \neq 0$, the
SEED is given the value n; if $n = 0$, it is given
the value of another system variable (called
FRAMES) that counts the frames so far
displayed on the television, and so should be
fairly random.
Error B occurs if n is not in the range 0 to
65535.

REM ...   No effect. '...' can be any sequence of characters except **ENTER**.

RETURN

Pops a line number from the **GOSUB** stack and jumps to the line after it.
Error 7 occurs when there is no line number on the stack. There is some mistake in your program; **GOSUB**s are not properly balanced by **RETURN**s.

RUN

RUN Ø

RUN n

CLEAR, and then **GOTO** n.

SAVE f

Records the program and variables on tape and calls it f.
SAVE should not be used inside a **GOSUB** routine.
Error F occurs if f is the empty string, which is not allowed.

SCROLL

Scrolls the display file up one line, losing the top line and making an empty line at the bottom.
Note that the new line is genuinely empty with just an **ENTER** character and no spaces.

SLOW

Puts the computer into compute and display mode, in which the display file is displayed continuously and computing is done during the spaces at the top and bottom of the picture.

STOP

Stops the program with Report 9. **CONT** will resume with the following line.

UNPLOT m,n

Like **PLOT**, but blanks out a pixel instead of blacking it in.

APPENDIX H
The System Variables

Reprinted from Timex *User Manual* by permission of Timex Computer Corporation

The System Variables

The bytes in memory from 16384 to 16508 are set aside for specific uses by the system. You can peek them to find out various things about the system, and some of them can be usefully poked. They are listed here with their uses.

These are called system variables and carry names, but do not confuse them with the variables used by the BASIC. You cannot use the names in a BASIC program; they are simply mnemonics that are used to make it easier to refer to the variables.

The abbreviations in column 1 have the following meanings.

X   The variable should not be poked, because the system might crash.
N   Poking the variable will have no lasting affect.
S   The variable is saved by **SAVE**.

The number in column 1 is the number of bytes in the variable. For two bytes, the first one is the *less* significant byte — the reverse of what you might expect. So to poke a value v to a two-byte variable at address n, use

POKE n,v−256***INT** (v/256)
POKE n+1,**INT** (v/256)

and to peek its value, use the expression:

PEEK n + 256***PEEK** (n+1)

Notes	Address	Name	Contents
1	16384	ERR_NR	1 less than the report code. Starts off at 255 (for −1), so **PEEK** 16384, if it works at all, gives 255. **POKE** 16384, n can be used to force an error halt: Ø $<=$ n $<=$ 14 gives one of the usual reports, 15 $<=$ n $<=$ 34 or 99 $<=$ n $<=$ 127 gives a nonstandard report, and 35 $<=$ n $<=$ 98 is likely to mess up the display file.
X1	16385	FLAGS	Various flags to control the BASIC system.
X2	16386	ERR_SP	Address of first item on machine stack (after **GOSUB** returns).
2	16388	RAMTOP	Address of first byte above BASIC system area. You can poke this to make **NEW** reserve space above that area (see Chapter 25) or to fool **CLS** into setting up a minimal display file (Chapter 26).
N1	16390	MODE	Specifies K, L, F or G cursor
N2	16391	PPC	Line number of statement currently being executed. Poking this has no lasting effect except in the last line of the program.
S1	16393	VERSN	Ø Identifies 8K ROM in saved programs.
S2	16394	E_PPC	Number of current line (with program cursor).
SX2	16396	D_FILE	See Chapter 26.
S2	16398	DF_CC	Address of **PRINT** position in display file. Can be poked so that **PRINT** output is sent elsewhere.
SX2	16400	VARS	See Chapter 26.
SN2	16402	DEST	Address of variable in assignment.
SX2	16404	E_LINE	See Chapter 26.
SX2	16406	CH_ADD	Address of the next character to be interpreted: the character after the argument of **PEEK**, or the **ENTER** at the end of a **POKE** statement.
S2	16408	X_PTR	Address of the character preceding the marker.

Notes	Address	Name	Contents
SX2	16410	STKBOT	See Chapter 26.
SX2	16412	STKEND	
SN1	16414	BREG	Calculator's b register.
SN2	16415	MEM	Address of area used for calculator's memory. (Usually MEMOT, but not always.)
S1	16417	not used	
SX1	16418	DF_SZ	The number of lines (including one blank line) in the lower part of the screen.
S2	16419	S_TOP	The number of the top program line in automatic listings.
SN2	16421	LAST_K	Shows which keys pressed
SN1	16423		Debounce status of keyboard.
SN1	16424	MARGIN	Number of blank lines above or below picture — 31.
SX2	16425	NXTLIN	Address of next program line to be executed.
S2	16427	OLDPPC	Line number to which **CONT** jumps.
SN1	16429	FLAGX	Various flags.
SN2	16430	STRLEN	Length of string type designation in assignment.
SN2	16432	T-ADDR	Address of next item in syntax table (very unlikely to be useful).
S2	16434	SEED	The seed for **RND**. This is the variable that is set by **RAND**.
S2	16436	FRAMES	Counts the frames displayed on the television. Bit 15 is 1. Bits Ø to 14 are decremented for each frame sent to the television. This can be used for timing, but **PAUSE** also uses it. **PAUSE** resets bit 15 to Ø and puts in bits Ø to 14 the length of the pause. When these have been counted down to zero, the pause stops. If the pause stops because of a key depression, bit 15 is set to one again.
S1	16438	COORDS	x-coordinate of last point **PLOT**ted.
S1	16439		y-coordinate of the last point **PLOT**ted.
S1	16440	PR_CC	Less significant byte of address of next position for **LPRINT** to print at (in PRBUFF).
SX1	16441	S_POSN	Column number for **PRINT** position.
SX1	16442		Line number for **PRINT** position.
S1	16443	CDFLAG	Various flags. Bit 7 is on (1) during compute and display e.

Notes	Address	Name	Contents
S33	16444	PRBUFF	Printer buffer (33rd character) is **ENTER**.
SN30	16477	MEMBOT	Calculator's memory area; used to store numbers that cannot conveniently be put on the calculator stack.
S2	16507	not used	

Exercises

1. Try this program

```
10 FOR N=0 TO 21
20 PRINT PEEK (PEEK 16400+256* PEEK 16401 + N)
30 NEXT N
```

This tells you the first 22 bytes of the variables area: try to match up the control variable N with the description in Chapter 26.

2. In the program above, change line 20 to

```
20 PRINT PEEK (16509+N)
```

This tells you the first 22 bytes of the program area. Match these up with the program itself.

INDEX

Que Microcomputer Products

Title	Item No.	Date Available
BOOKS:		
Apple II Pocket Dictionary	0-88022-023-6	Early '83
Apple II Word Processing	0-88022-005-8	Currently
C Programming Language	0-88022-022-8	Spring '83
CP/M Word Processing	0-88022-006-6	Currently
IBM PC Expansion & Software Guide	0-88022-019-8	Currently
IBM PC Pocket Dictionary	0-88022-024-4	Early '83
IBM's Personal Computer-hbk.	0-88022-101-1	Currently
IBM's Personal Computer-pbk.	0-88022-100-3	Currently
The Osborne Portable Computer	0-88022-015-5	Dec. '82
SuperCalc;SuperModels for Business	0-88022-007-4	Nov. '82
Timex/Sinclair 1000 User's Guide	0-88022-016-3	Currently
VisiCalc Models for Business	0-88022-017-1	Dec. '82
SOFTWARE:		
CalcSheets for Business	1100 Series	Dec. '82

"CalcSheets for business" is a series of VisiCalc and SuperCalc models to assist businesspeople in cash management, debt management, fixed asset management, working capital management, and other business management. These models run on the IBM Personal Computer, Apple II computer and other popular personal computers.

Que Timex/Sinclair 1000 Books

Timex/Sinclair 1000 User's Guide (Volume I)   (this book)

Timex/Sinclair 1000 User's Guide (Volume II)   Available: December '82

Timex/Sinclair 1000 Pocket Dictionary   Available: Early '83

Timex/Sinclair 1000 Games   Available: Spring '83

Notes

Notes

Notes

Notes

Notes

Notes

Notes

Notes

Notes